Malice Aforethought

Malice Aforethought

How Lawyers Use Our Secret Rules to Get Rich, Get Sex, Get Even . . . and Get Away with It

David W. Marston

William Morrow and Company, Inc.
New York

It is the policy of William Morrow and Company, Inc., and its imprints and affiliates, recognizing the importance of preserving what has been written, to print the books we publish on acid-free paper, and we exert our best efforts to that end.

Library of Congress Cataloging-in-Publication Data

Marston, David W., 1942–
Malice aforethought : how lawyers use our secret rules to get rich, get sex, get even—and get away with it / David W. Marston.
p. cm.
ISBN 0-688-07705-6
1. Legal ethics—United States—Anecdotes. 2. Practice of law—United States—Corrupt practices—Anecdotes. 3. Judicial corruption—United States—Anecdotes. I. Title.
K184.M37 1991
174'.3—dc20 90-46396
CIP

Printed in the United States of America

First Edition

1 2 3 4 5 6 7 8 9 10

BOOK DESIGN BY MARK STEIN STUDIOS

Preface

I think it was when they convicted "Mugsy" that it first occurred to me that I knew a lot of lawyers in jail or trouble.

Actually, Mugsy's misfortune was not altogether surprising, since his schoolboy reputation as a clowning cut-up had endured through college and law school; even after years in practice, Philadelphia criminal defense lawyer Joseph Montgomery was still "Mugsy" to everyone who knew him.

Funny, engaging, master of flash and brash, Montgomery knew his way around the courthouse. He had worked as an assistant district attorney, then switched to defense. It would not have been a shock to hear that Mugsy sometimes cut a legal corner, maybe slipping '76ers tickets to a court clerk, for example, or winking as he helped a client remember a shaky alibi.

But it was a jolt to learn that he had been convicted of

involvement with a drug ring that had moved $70 million worth of methamphetamine, more than half a ton. For that, a federal judge sentenced Montgomery to four years in prison and a $10,000 fine.

(Mugsy said he'd been framed.)

That was in 1986, as I approached my twentieth year in the legal profession. During that time, I had engaged in the law business in half a dozen different positions, three in the public sector, three private. It was a career path that had not qualified me for any gold watches, but had exposed me to an unusual cross-section of the profession.

Fresh out of Harvard Law School and back from a tour as legal/gunnery officer on a Navy frigate, I had started practice with Montgomery, McCracken, Walker & Rhoads, a venerable white-shoe Philadelphia firm. A dignified portrait of former United States Supreme Court Justice Owen J. Roberts, a onetime Montgomery, McCracken partner, graced the elegant reception area. But the character of the firm had been molded by Colonel C. Brewster Rhoads, hero in *two* wars, bar association leader, nationally known trial lawyer, and charismatic paterfamilias until the day he died at age eighty.

While he lived, the colonel presided over an orderly world. Gentlemen wore white shirts and dark somber suits and observed certain unwritten rules in dealing with each other. For example, in the usage of the telephone (a suspect instrument, since it could without warning allow persons wearing shirts of many colors to communicate directly with gentlemen), the colonel had a rigid code: Calls from clients must be returned, without exception, on the day received; calls from brother practitioners, within the hour; and calls from judges must be taken at once (or, if nature prevented that, returned within ten minutes).

But even as the colonel passed down the rules, it was clear that gentlemen were becoming an endangered species. The newly hired lawyers in our group included the firm's first Jew, first black, and a handful of other recent graduates with dubious table manners and no social connections. We were more likely to have worked parking cars at debutante parties than to have dated the debs. We could learn to do whatever it was that Montgomery, McCracken lawyers did, but it was not going to be the same.

While I was learning corporate law during the day and also doing occasional criminal defense, my legal education lurched along at night in a less formal venue, usually the Parkway Room, sometimes the Fireside Tavern or Chickie's in Chinatown. Those downtown bars were the regular haunts of Judge Edward T. Quinn. Judge Quinn—Quinnie to his many friends—was a judge but *not* a lawyer; an old-school, yarn-spinning, whiskey-drinking, wake-attending politician who had been elected magistrate before a reform movement had somehow convinced the voters that the one credential judges ought to have was a law degree.

Once the lawyer-magistrates came in, most of the old-timers were relegated to night court to serve out their terms. Judge Quinn viewed this assignment as simply one more injustice inflicted upon him by reformers, and so made certain that his judicial duties did not significantly intrude on his regular evening routine of taproom visits around the city.

My original reason for joining the judge on his nocturnal rounds was to get his blessing, as de facto political boss in our neighborhood, of my effort to win local office. After ruminating on that unwelcome proposal for several weeks, he finally conceded: "Well, I've lost with a black, lost with a Jew, lost with an Irishman, might as well try a WASP." (He lost again.)

But I continued to stop by the Parkway Room occasionally, simply because I liked the judge and his colorful scene, enjoyed listening to his old stories, and watching the job seekers, ticket fixers, hustlers—and lawyers—who would send a drink over to Quinnie to open a conversation.

By the time the conversations ended, the lawyers often ended up buying more than a drink. Sometimes it would be a book of raffle tickets to help buy a new car for the nuns, or uniforms for the local basketball team, or it might be a promise to represent someone in the neighborhood who needed a lawyer and couldn't afford to pay. No one ever balked, because the judge had built a lot of law practices.

Barry Denker understood this right away. Denker was a young lawyer just getting started, trying to figure out how things worked in City Hall. It did not take him long to realize that the same judge who could free criminal defendants on bail at 2:00 A.M. could also make suggestions about which lawyer they should retain to beat the rap altogether. The judge would not tell the defendant directly, of course, but word could get around.

I don't know exactly what word might have gotten around, but I do recall the judge mentioning once that Barry Denker had sent him a case of whiskey at Christmas.

After a few years, I moved on to a different form of legal education, joining the Washington staff of U.S. Senator Richard S. Schweiker of Pennsylvania (one of the minority of nonlawyers in that deliberative body). As legislative counsel, I analyzed and tracked proposed legislation, staffed Senate debates, met with constituent groups, and generally enjoyed the unpredictable variety that makes the Senate staff a fascinating experience.

But the Washington centerpiece, while I was there, was Watergate. I remember unpacking the television first when I arrived in June 1973, because the Watergate hearings were just starting. By the time they ended, it was pretty clear that something must be fundamentally wrong in our profession, since a parade of the most powerful, influential lawyers in the country, including the attorney general of the United States, had been convicted of crimes.

But the political scandal largely obscured the professional one, and it was easy to dismiss the attorney misdeeds as being *caused* by "Watergate," like that might be some sort of virus.

If it was a virus, though, it was clearly contagious beyond Washington, as I discovered when I returned to Philadelphia after being named by President Gerald R. Ford to be United States attorney. Our office convicted a number of powerful lawmakers—many of them lawyers—in corruption probes, including the speaker of the Pennsylvania House of Representatives, the potent chairman of the Pennsylvania Senate Appropriations Committee, and dozens of other officials in both parties. And as federal prosecutor, I spent a lot of time with criminal defense attorneys, and sometimes heard snatches of lawyer gossip about Barry Denker.

He was fast emerging as one of the most flamboyant—and busiest—defense lawyers in town. There were tales that he wore full-length fur coats and cowboy boots to court, he was often seen driving expensive sports cars, and rumor had it that he handled something like five hundred criminal cases a year. In short, he seemed to have figured out how things worked in City Hall.

After leaving the prosecutor's office, I hung up my shingle as a sole practitioner. Although rapidly expanding megafirms have dominated recent legal headlines, fully half of all lawyers in America still practice the old-fashioned way: in solo practice, or firms with fewer than five attorneys. It's a world away from the Big Firms, where lawyers often have carbon-copy credentials, wardrobes, work habits, and billing rates.

The world of small firms and solo practitioners is much zestier. Its bag of barristers is thoroughly mixed, some operating out of opulent offices, brilliantly successful, others using the bar association library as a base and barely hanging on. And like anyone who starts his own small business, solo practitioners have the satisfaction of knowing, when they turn off the lights each night, that the enterprise that has been created is theirs.

They also know that if they forget to turn off the lights or to water the plants or to buy typewriter ribbons or to get a copy of that recent Supreme Court opinion or to do any of a hundred other routine tasks—no one else is going to do it for them.

It was fun.

But after five years, the limitations of practicing alone came to outweigh the fun. The Pittsburgh-based firm of Buchanan Ingersoll had adopted an aggressive strategy in order to build a statewide practice in Pennsylvania, and I joined that firm, as partner in charge of the Philadelphia office.

That was about the time they convicted Joe Montgomery, which was when I decided to sit down and figure out how many of my lawyer acquaintances had ended up in trouble.

Ellis Cook made my list.

We had been classmates and friends from grade school, and I had a clear recollection of him as a happy camper on Boy Scout trips, a roly-poly kid who matured into a solid, hardworking teenager with lots of friends. Our high school yearbook called him "a medium tank—armed with shoulder pads and sheer determination . . . a thinking man and rugged individual . . . law to come."

The law did come, but not the way Ellis expected. It came in the form of FBI agents masquerading as Arab sheiks to sting a string of political fixers, in the undercover ABSCAM investigation. The most memorable on-camera performances in that drama were turned in by a Florida congressman gleefully stuffing his pockets with cash and Congressman Michael "Ozzie" Myers of Philadelphia, who explained "Money talks, bullshit walks" to an undercover agent.

But Ellis Cook, my friend from Boy Scout days and by

then a partner in a small Philadelphia firm, also had a role. He posed as a federal immigration official in an effort to get thousands of dollars from an Arab sheik (who, in turn, was actually an undercover FBI agent).

Cook promptly returned the money. He was never indicted, but instead received a federal grant of immunity; his testimony helped convict other ABSCAM defendants. But he was suspended from the practice of law, and eventually withdrew from the profession.

Then there was Peter Stern, also an acquaintance from high school. Peter was a brilliant student who graduated cum laude from the University of Pennsylvania Law School and went on to become a partner in one of Philadelphia's largest firms. As the years flipped past, I saw him rarely but heard about him often, as he became a prominent Philadelphia labor lawyer.

A busy practitioner who favored dark pin-striped suits, Stern was also active in civic, religious, and professional activities. By his own account, he was on the "fast track" in his law firm.

It was too fast.

Stern was charged with having made an illegal $5,000 cash payoff to a Teamsters Union official, and disbarred by the Pennsylvania Supreme Court in 1987.

And Herman Bloom, whom I knew from politics, drew jail time in 1989 for making cash kickbacks to his client, the rough-and-tumble Roofers Union Local 30-30B—which, as we'll see, used the cash to pay off Philadelphia judges on a wholesale basis.

As my personal list of lawyer acquaintances in trouble grew longer, I learned that the American Bar Association—while not advertising it—also has a list of attorneys who have been subject to professional discipline. It's a single-spaced computer printout, one line for each Bad Lawyer.

The ABA list is two football fields long, 602 feet. Put

another way, the ABA printout has 649 pages, 49 names to a page, which means that if someone decided to lay out the disciplined lawyers end-to-end, the result would be more than thirty miles of bad lawyers

My guess was that the lawyers on the ABA list would probably be a lot like those on my list. The disciplined lawyers would not appear to be evil people—more likely, they would be normal-looking lawyers (or ex-lawyers) who, in a casual meeting, you might well choose to represent you. This hunch was confirmed as I learned that, in the overwhelming majority of cases recorded on the ABA list, regardless of what crime had been committed, other lawyers were willing to stand up and testify under oath—without winking—that the Bad Lawyer was of good personal and professional character.

In short, when lawyers reflect on friends who have had a professional problem, or read about strangers in other places who have been disciplined or disbarred . . . well, the bad guys can look a lot like us.

This book is about Bad Lawyers.

Everyone in practice knows lawyers who have been subject to professional discipline, and other lawyers—generally many more—who should have been but weren't.

We prefer to keep these secrets within the profession—bad for business to talk about them. Certainly, we'll acknowledge the handful of misbehaving attorneys who make headlines in our respective communities, no choice there, but we'd like the thousands of others across the country to stay below the surface, invisible. And since we regulate and discipline ourselves, almost always behind a shroud of secrecy, we can make sure they do.

The idea of this book is to let the public in on these professional secrets. We'll see how often lawyers break the law and trample ethical rules, who their victims are, and what kinds of punishments result—or don't. This account will trace the temptations lawyers face in everyday practice, and explain why—when lawyers yield to temptation—the rules of professional conduct are often a Bad Lawyer's best friend. We'll also see how lawyers convicted of felonies can still be in good professional standing—and how seemingly innocent conduct can turn into a violation of the lawyer rules.

A number of respected scholars, including Stephen Gillers of New York University Law School, Geoffrey Hazard at Yale, and Charles Wolfram at Cornell, have specialized in the study of legal ethics.

I'm certainly not an expert in this technical field. But after two decades of lawyering, I feel qualified to look around our profession and say what I've seen. Understanding what Bad Lawyers are up to, it seems to me, is the starting point for running them out of the legal business.

But let's not prejudge.

It may turn out that Bad Lawyers are actually good, and the only problem is that the public does not understand what lawyers are *supposed* to do.

In that case, we'll jump in to defend them.

No problem.

We switch sides all the time, we can do it in a New York minute.

A note on approach: Since the effort here is to paint a *current* picture of the legal profession, the focus will be on what lawyers have been up to recently, with most examples being drawn from within the last decade. That may not seem so recent to lay readers, but lawyers track time a little differently from everyone else, sort of the reverse of the way dogs age. The barrister knows a ten-year-old case is young. Chances are, it will be reversed by another court at some point in the future, or at least modified or distinguished. Lawyers like cases to be older than they are, tried and tested over time.

For that reason, we'll also make reference to a couple

of more mature cases, specifically the 1883 Supreme Court decision involving "One John, Otherwise Unknown," and also the case, over two hundred years ago, in which Lord Mansfield set forth the purpose of lawyer discipline.

Also, even though "lawyer" and "attorney" have different technical meanings, they are used here interchangeably (with an occasional "barrister" or "counselor" sprinkled in for variety). And without any defensible reason, the masculine pronoun is used throughout (which may make this one of the last accounts by a member of the disappearing tribe of male lawyers, since women now predominate in many graduating law school classes).

Finally, much of this account is in the first person, to emphasize that *everyone* in the legal profession has a part in lawyer misconduct.

Wait . . . that's not right.

I never broke the rules.

Maybe not.

Most of us have never personally stolen money or fixed cases or dealt drugs.

But neither have we confronted the lawyers who do engage in misconduct and chased them out of our profession.

Like, for example, Barry Denker.

When whispers swept through the Philadelphia legal community a couple of years ago that Denker had gotten jammed up on a case and ended up wearing a wire, cooperating with the feds, lots of City Hall lawyers and judges got extremely nervous.

And Judge Kenny Harris was more than nervous. He had done a lot of business with Denker over the years, good for both of them, but he knew there was at least a chance that some of the rough stuff he had said might have been picked up on tape.

Like when he had instructed his courtroom deputy to go see the "fuckin' big fat Jew" and get a payoff. That statement, it turned out, came across loud and clear on the surveillance tape. Judge Harris was later convicted on corruption charges and sentenced to twelve years in prison.

But if judges and lawyers in City Hall were nervous, once they heard Barry Denker was in trouble, no one was surprised. Even after Denker sent a batch of lawyers and judges to jail with his testimony about two decades of fixing cases, there were no reported incidents of Philadelphia lawyers keeling over in astonishment.

Because we knew it all along.

Not specifics.

We didn't know exactly what Denker would *say* to a judge as he fixed a case—until we read the transcripts of his secretly recorded conversation with Judge Herbert R. Cain:

"Here's five and I'll get you a thousand on Monday afternoon after it's over for this guy, 'cause I've got people gonna pay all right."

(On Monday, Cain made a ruling that forced the district attorney to withdraw the case; Judge Cain was later convicted of extortion.)

But every lawyer working in City Hall had a fairly accurate idea how Barry Denker practiced.

And like our lawyer colleagues across the country who practice daily with their own Barry Denkers, we looked the other way.

Denker, by the way, does not have much use for his full-length fur coat these days. After testifying against the judges who took his bribes, he moved to sunny Albuquerque, New Mexico, where he used the cash the feds gave him for cooperating to open the Black Swan Gallery, an upscale art store. In 1989, Denker moved again, this time to federal prison, to serve the year and a day sentence he recieved for bribery.

Contents

Malice aforethought. The intentional doing of an unlawful act which was determined upon before it was executed.

—*State* v. *Lane*, 371 S.W.2d 261, 263 (1963)

They're Everywhere!

At first glance, the crimes seem unconnected, random threads that fit no pattern.

They occur at different times, in widely scattered locations around the world. In most cases, investigators would quickly identify them as professional jobs, but find no obvious evidence linking the perpetrators—who seem to be unacquainted with each other.

- A high roller in New York, well known to local police, skims more than $800,000 from a union retirement fund, and loses it all in Atlantic City gambling sprees. On the surface, it's probable that he's connected, somehow, but the usual mob informants draw a blank.
- In Washington, D.C., a man named Fortunato Mendes is charged with distributing cocaine, not usually a free-lance activity at the street level. Before his drug case comes to trial, he also is charged with murder.

- In Chicago, a former fashion model tells the grand jury that she has been the mistress of a man named Michael Guinan, and describes his lavish gifts to her. A short time later, in a late-night panic, she calls former U.S. Congressman Barry Goldwater, Jr., a close friend, and says she is frightened about cooperating in the probe of Guinan.

  No one has seen the model since.

  Six months later, Guinan, registered under a phony name and carrying two guns and $33,500 in cash, is arrested in San Diego.

- A Honolulu man hires local crime figure Maka Tuli Toomata to kill a competitor. But the scheme unravels, and Toomata warns the target, who alerts the police.

What the Honolulu police discover, however, is the same thing authorities have found in other cities. These crimes, and hundreds more, are indeed connected: The perpetrators all belong to the same organization.

They all have undergone the same tough initiation, and once admitted to membership, all have sworn the same oath. They live by their own rules and have fiercely resisted efforts by outsiders to penetrate their clan. They have a code of silence that makes the Mafia's dreaded *omertà* seem gossipy.

And while the organization rigidly limits the operations of its members to their assigned turf, their criminal activities within these areas are surprisingly varied.

- A Long Island member targets potential robbery victims, one of whom is also raped and sodomized, for the Colombo crime family, while a member in New Jersey is part of a ring that moves $200 million worth of amphetamines over a three-year period, netting $3.5 million in drug profits.

- In Chicago, an FBI dragnet snags nearly four dozen members in a major corruption probe; they are convicted of bribing fifteen city judges.

- Although men traditionally have run the action, women are increasingly involved. In Tennessee, one of the organization's women manages to slip a gun to a two-time killer and spring him from prison; in South Carolina, another grabs $1,819 from the sale of Girl Scout cookies.

The organization enforces its own discipline, and outsiders can piece together only the most fragmentary picture of the process. But while hard statistics about crime and misconduct by members remain elusive, there has unquestionably been a sharp escalation in recent years. And while most members prefer to work alone or in small, close-knit groups, often run by family members who have been in the organization for generations, the cash they generate, estimated by some officials to be more than $40 billion a year, would put the organization comfortably in the Fortune 500.

In every state, the organization has tentacles that reach into the legislature, as well as intimate knowledge of the local criminal justice system. Laws that might threaten operations are vigorously opposed, and when memers are convicted of crimes, punishments are often lenient. The New Jersey member in the amphetaine ring, for example, paid a $5,000 fine (plus three years' probation and two years of community service) for his part in producing $3.5 million in drug profits.

Likewise, a New York member who pleaded guilty to embezzling more than $250,000 was sent to jail for ninety days by a judge who announced he was sending a "warning" to other criminals.

Aside from soft punishments, there is one other key perk that comes with membership: After criminal convictions, even for serious felonies, members often go right back to work in the organization.

It's not the Mafia.

Not the Medellín drug cartel, or some shadowy Chinese tong.

The members are all lawyers.

And the organization is the American legal profession.

So what?

When attorneys start tossing around Latin phrases, you can listen a long time without hearing *mea culpa*. That is not because we're arrogant or lack basic human feelings (indeed, as we'll see, there are plenty of those human feelings among the attorney population). Rather, it's because our legal training all cuts the other way. We don't get stampeded by a few lurid headlines; we're trained to consider *every* side of an issue, to carefully weigh all available evidence before drawing any conclusions.

It's not surprising, then, that there's no panic in the profession over a few examples—even splashy ones—of misconduct by lawyers. We look at our world a little differently than you might.

In the first place, there are something like 850,000 lawyers in this country—how excited are we supposed to get if a few dozen misbehave? Indeed, any group that size, professional or otherwise, will include at least as many bad actors. All this tells you about the law is that the law of averages works.

If someone *really* wants to know what's going on in any organization as large and diverse as the legal profession, the sensible way to find out is to check with its top official. In the law business, that's the president of the American Bar Association (ABA). That position is held by a different lawyer each year, but a recent ABA president, Eugene C. Thomas, was not afraid to address the sensitive issue of professional misconduct.

"We are the best disciplined profession in the world," Thomas admitted (take *that*, Marines) in a 1987 letter to the *Bar Leader*, "and our achievements outmatch those of any organization concerned with honesty, public service, and the delivery of competent representation to a class of clients."

(Hmmmm. Does that mean we just outmatched ourselves? I mean, who else is *in* the business of delivering representation to clients? Well, maybe social workers.)

While Thomas's statement would not appear to leave much room for argument, it actually was part of an argument, since it was made in response to a lawyer-written article about professional misconduct titled "The Discipline Pendulum: Interest in Reform on the Downswing." That article also appeared in the *Bar Leader*—which, adding irony to insult, is published by the ABA.

(President Thomas seemed to think this was about like Tass taking a shot at Mikhail Gorbachev pre-*glasnost*. He opened his letter: "If you have a Letters to the Editor column, I should like this published. It is a little unique because I am the President of the American Bar Association, the sponsoring entity responsible for your publication.")

(In case you missed it, this is a lawyer's subtle way of saying, I don't read your rag but I own your ass. Since Thomas didn't pull the plug on the *Bar Leader*, though, he should have tossed in the old but-I'll-defend-to-the-death-your-right-to-say-it, just to keep the editors relaxed.)

But even if there are a few quibblers, most lawyers do not lose sleep worrying about colleagues who may be breaking ethical rules, or clients who complain about it.

"We are addressing such concerns," ABA President Thomas assured lawyers, "through the new Standing Committee on Lawyer Competence, through the new Special Coordinating Committee on Professionalism, and through the revitalized efforts of our long-standing committees and groups working in the traditional fields of ethics and professional discipline."

Sounds good to us.

After all, it's important to keep this in historical perspective.

Since Moses brought the Ten Commandments down

from the mountain, the belief that both the law and lawyers are both full of tricks has been universal, and enduring. It's an impression that goes with the trade, transcending national boundaries and legal systems. And we know that if tricky blurs into bad, that suits lots of clients just fine.

"No lawyer is as bad as the client wants him to be," respected Washington attorney Jacob Stein told a reporter. The plain fact is that most clients want a shoot-to-kill gunslinger, a cold-blooded mouthpiece, the badder the better.

Even so, clients are quick to criticize lawyers, whether for high fees or low ethics, gutter tactics or bad results. We accept this. After all, in an adversary system that produces only winners and losers, we know we can't please anyone.

Anyone? How about the winners?

No, the winners always attribute victory to the inherent purity of their position, and blame the barrister for not somehow preventing them from being dragged into court in the first place. The occasional plaintiff who hits the jackpot with a monster verdict may, briefly, have a warm feeling for his attorney, but that generally cools off about the time the damage award check arrives—minus the lawyer's 30–40-percent fee, lopped off the top.

But if public grumbling has generally accompanied the practice of law, we pay about as much attention to it as to the Muzak in our elevators. Background noise, we're used to it. Understanding that, lawyers respond to critics and complainers in the same way they always have:

We ignore them.

Adolf Hitler would be entitled to a vigorous legal defense in America; everyone is, and attorneys know that if they do their job well—especially for bad clients—that will make more enemies than friends. Kids in grade school learn that Andrew Hamilton did the right thing by defending unpopular printer Peter Zenger in 1735, and flashy Melvin

Belli updated this lesson for the twentieth century in 1963, representing Jack Ruby after he gunned down President Kennedy's apparent killer, Lee Harvey Oswald.

Lawyers are devoted to these principles, so much so that we generally assume that *any* criticism is a result of our having taken a brave stand on some unpopular issue. That means that consumer complaints often register with us as a badge of professional courage; if you feel like you're not getting through when you disagree with your attorney, you're probably right.

In short, by the time they've practiced long enough to afford those flashy sharkskin suits, attorneys often have thick shark skins underneath too.

The bottom line is that with everyone else carping about lawyers, lawyers are more concerned about the bottom line. The legal profession may not be perfect, but top-end *starting* pay—for kids fresh out of law school—is $82,000 per year and rocketing higher.

Not bad.

And that salary seems almost modest, once you learn that a partner's slice of pie, in the firms paying that much to associates, is a tasty $700,000 a year. Oh, that's the *average* share, by the way; big hitters do a lot better.

Of course, only a tiny fraction of the profession is paid like that, we're quick to emphasize; maybe 10 percent or so in Big Firms, and the elite among plaintiff's lawyers. Still, if there are only a few at the top, the bottom can't be too far below, since the average lawyer income, across the board, is over $100,000.

Critics like Derek C. Bok complain that the profession's emphasis on squeezing out the last nickel in profits has also dried up its traditional *pro bono publico* services for clients who cannot pay, and priced legal services out of reach for many. The result, says Bok, is "far too much law for those who can afford it and far too little for those who cannot."

Odd that Bok should be second-guessing, though, since he was not exactly standing on the sidelines watching this thing shape up, but is the former dean of Harvard Law School.

Anyway, all that criticism stings less after a few trips to the bank, and there's no heavy lifting. On balance, lawyers know they've got a good thing going, and not many want to spoil it.

So even if we happen to see Bad Lawyers at the scene of a crime, the unspoken code of the Club says speak no evil.

The actual rules of the profession, which we'll call the Secret Rules, say the opposite. But the Rules don't get in the way much, since most lawyers could guess your Social Security number quicker than they could guess what Rule 8.3—or any other rule—of the Rules of Professional Conduct requires. (8.3 says that lawyers should blow the whistle on a Bad Lawyer if his conduct raises a "substantial" question about his fitness; more about that later).

But if lawyers are a little hazy on the ethical rules and downright squeamish about reporting misconduct, we don't see that as a big problem, because we don't imagine lawyers misbehave that often.

There's an occasional case, certainly, such as that of Pennsylvania attorney Jeffrey M. Silow, who revised the will of his millionaire client, Rose Weissman—after she had died.

And there was Florida lawyer Peter T. Roman. Attorney Roman wasn't tempted to play tricks with his client's will, since she died without one. Instead, he forged an affidavit naming a phony heir, then grabbed the lady's assets for himself.

And on the bizarre side, California lawyer Victor R. Lawhorn wanted to be sure that his estranged wife could not freeze the client funds in his attorney trust account, so he froze them himself—in his refrigerator. He kept his clients' cash cold in a "stash box" that looked like a Pepsi can; for commingling funds, the state disciplinary board suspended his license to practice for two years.

But nothing new here.

Sharp practices, unfortunately, have always been a problem on the fringes of the profession. Some down-and-out hack dips into a client escrow, an alcoholic attorney backdates a document, that sort of thing, impossible to stamp out completely. But it's certainly not a mainstream problem for the legal profession.

In most cases, the Bad Lawyers are quickly caught, and we're confident—although most of us don't have any firsthand experience with it—that professional discipline is swift and uncompromising. Good character, after all, is an absolute prerequisite to being a lawyer; that's one of the first things every new lawyer has to establish before being admitted to the bar.

Which, happily, is also the last time anyone checks up on it.

"Are you going to do it so that they don't find the body?" Paul Mostman asked his contract killer.

The killer shrugged.

"It's probably better if it isn't found," Mostman added (which must have left the killer shaking his head, thinking, "No shit").

Paul Mostman was a lawyer.

The person he was trying to kill was his client. He never got that done, because his hit man was working undercover for the cops, but he went far enough to write a check, paying for the hit.

Nevertheless, lawyer disciplinary authorities in the state where Mostman practiced, California, apparently thought he had a good reason for wanting to have his client killed, since they concluded that Mostman did not have the one flaw Bad Lawyers fear most: Moral Turpitude.

So even though Mostman spent a year in the slammer for his abortive effort, the Golden State bar panel recommended "a severe sanction," which came out to three years of supervised probation. (Hey, we're talking California.)

When this decision was reviewed by the California Supreme Court in 1989, however, the court must have concluded that there were just too many serious threats to ignore. Referring to his client, attorney Mostman had been secretly recorded saying he wanted to "hurt him bad." Then he toughened up, saying "I'd rather *off* him, you know," and also that he had "no compunction against doing it," except for "repercussions."

If that's not Moral Turpitude, what is?

(As we'll see, no one knows—which is the whole idea.)

We should mention, at this point, that the lawyer-client relationship is often complex, even close to a love-hate affair. We love getting paid, but hate messy problems and crazy midnight calls (which is what they pay us for). Even so, no matter what his client may have done, attorney Mostman's behavior was pretty extreme, which forced the California Supreme Court to reverse the bar panel, and to conclude that Mostman did in fact have the big MT, Moral Turpitude.

But the court was still pretty relaxed about Mostman's hit scheme (which might have sent him to the gas chamber, if it had worked out), ruling that he should only be suspended from practice for a brief two years.

(Once that's over and he's back in business, clients would be smart to give Mostman plenty of room.)

Because California has more lawyers than any other state (indeed, more than most *countries*—China, for example, has about 33,000 lawyers for a population of 1.1 billion; California has more than three times that many), and also because its professional disciplinary system is one of the country's most advanced, Mostman's misadventure might help reconcile the two clashing pictures we've seen so far:

Is there a runaway crime wave sweeping the legal profession, with Bad Lawyers mixed up in everything from drugs to extortion to murder—and often still in good standing in the legal Club?

Or, as lawyers generally see the picture, is it really business as usual, with only a few bad actors bending the rules, about like they have throughout history?

If Mostman is at all typical, lawyers seem to have advanced well beyond backdating documents and jiggling accounts. This conclusion is reinforced by the fact that, even though Mostman *paid to have his client killed,* neither the state disciplinary board nor the California Supreme Court was sufficiently shocked by that to toss him out of the law business permanently.

And a quick glance around the country confirms that lawyer misconduct has taken some imaginative turns.

- In Michigan, divorce lawyer Frederick Gold warned his new client that her estranged husband might assault her. She doubted it, but Gold persisted; he showed the client a photograph of a naked woman tied to a pole with her mouth taped, and suggested that her husband might do the same to her. He urged her to take off her clothes and let him snap some photographs, the old before-and-after trick, to prove she was uninjured when the divorce proceeding started.

  She finally did.

  Gold snapped off his shots, then he made sexual advances.

  The lawyers who discipline Michigan lawyers gave him a three-year suspension (which would seem to mean it's better to try to kill your client in California than to make moves on her in Michigan).

- Andrew Carter Thornton II discovered there was more money in smuggling cocaine from Colombia than in lawyering in Kentucky. How much more? When federal agents caught up with him, the attorney had $15 million worth of cocaine strapped to his body. Unfortunately, also strapped to attorney Thornton's body was a parachute that failed to open when the smuggler bailed out of a twin-engine Cessna over northwestern Tennessee.

- Philadelphia lawyer Fredric A. Shapiro incorporated a new title insurance agency, nothing sinister in that. But then he used that agency to churn out phony title reports showing that his townhouse/law office was owned free and clear, without any mortgage or other debts. Then, armed with a clean title report, he went to a bank and borrowed money, giving a mortgage on his property as security.

  That worked so smoothly he did it again. And again.

  Shapiro kept on doing it until he had run up a total of $8.6 million in fraudulent borrowings from ten banks. Then, drowning in interest charges, he went to the federal prosecutor and confessed.

- Crime-fighting Camden, New Jersey, prosecutor Samuel Asbell liked to show up at drug arrests wearing a mean-looking pistol in a shoulder holster and toting a sawed-off shotgun (which he described as "a real crowd pleaser"). Asbell's big guns saved him from near-certain assassination, when he was able to blast away and kill one of two assailants ("I saw his head explode," the lawman reported grimly) who had opened fire on his Lincoln Town Car from their own speeding vehicle.

  So he said.

  But no one could find the body with the exploded head, or the bad guys' car.

  After a few days of hot TV coverage, in which Asbell warned the nation about the perils of "narco-terrorism," he was arrested for filing a false police report. He later admitted that he had shot the windows out of his own car in the hoax, which was actually a play to get reappointed to office.

But even if lawyers are into big-time crime, what about professional discipline? Maybe Mostman got off easy, but what usually happens?

Usually, nothing.

When you file a complaint against your lawyer, in some

states you will *never* be told what, if anything, is done about it. But based on the numbers, if you don't hear, assume that the file it landed in was round.

In one recent year, for example, state disciplinary agencies around the country received a total of 93,622 complaints against lawyers. That same year, 2,817 lawyers were formally charged with misconduct, 541 were disbarred, and 2,274 attorneys received lesser discipline, ranging from suspension to public reprimand. (Those numbers are highly misleading, of course, because it usually takes many years to get from complaint to discipline, which means that the 541 lawyers disbarred were not even included in the 93,622 complaints). The ABA estimates that only two-tenths of a percent of all American lawyers are ever subject to professional discipline.

Lawyers have to love those odds.

Even in the rare cases when action is taken, and the disciplinary committee brings formal charges against a lawyer, in most states the hearings and deliberations—and even the name of the lawyer involved—are all kept secret. The only clue for the public is a single initial, since when the case is finally printed it will be titled, for example, "Attorney C. v. Office of Disciplinary Counsel."

Why?

"This rule [of secrecy] . . . reflects the considered judgment that there is nothing to be gained and much to be lost," one state court explained, "where an attorney's reputation and livelihood are concerned, by opening to the public the record of proceedings concerning allegations of professional misconduct which are ultimately found to be groundless."

Translated from the legalese: Bad Lawyers are for our eyes only.

And just to keep everyone guessing, each state has different rules. A proceeding that's public in Texas will be private in Oklahoma; attorney conduct considered ethical in one state can be taboo next door. The result: Any national statistics are virtually meaningless, since they inevitably compare bad apples and oranges.

There's another trick. In our version of Macy's-doesn't-tell-Gimbels, courts often won't permit the lawyer disciplinary boards in sister states to talk to each other.

Exhibit A: Pennsylvania officials recently discovered evidence that a lawyer who practiced in both New Jersey and Pennsylvania had "commingled and possibly misappropriated" funds of clients in both states.

Did the Pennsylvania lawyer disciplinary agency grab the phone and tell New Jersey, before any other clients could be ripped off?

Well, they tried to.

But attorney T. appealed to the Pennsylvania Supreme Court, which ruled that the Pennsylvania Office of Disciplinary Counsel could *not* share its evidence with Garden State authorities—even though New Jersey, under its own confidentiality rules, would have had to protect any secrets.

"Our rules of confidentiality are consistent with other states including New Jersey and the ABA Standards," the court ruled, "*none of which* provides for disclosure of disciplinary information to attorney disciplinary authorities in other states prior to adjudication."

In short, a lawyer on the professional ropes in one state, sometimes even disbarred, can practice away next door—and even lawyers in the discipline business may not be able to do anything about it.

The American Bar Association does publish a state-by-state summary of disciplinary actions taken against lawyers, but—as we'll see—it's full of large holes.

And, saving one of the best tricks for last, some states *suspend* disciplinary actions whenever a lawsuit is filed against the attorney, on the theory that the court case should take precedence.

That sounds reasonable—if you don't think it through.

But what it really means is, the badder the lawyer, the smaller his chances of getting disciplined anytime soon.

Assuming without deciding (that's a phrase we learn in law school that lets lawyers argue both sides of a question) that maybe there *is* a national epidemic of lawyer crime and misconduct, with professional discipline being haphazard at best, it's still not as bad as that sounds. There may be a lot of Bad Lawyers on the loose, but lawyers in practice know that misconduct is really concentrated in one specific area of the profession.

It's those flamboyant personal injury lawyers who really besmirch the profession, starchy Big-Firm lawyers grumble. They swoop down on disasters like vultures, sometimes even disguising their runners as Red Cross workers or priests to sign up clients. They fake injuries, then follow up with fictitious medical care. The pattern is so well established that every big-city transit agency expects that the number of "victims" who file lawsuits after every bus or subway accident will exceed the actual number of passengers by as much as 30 percent.

Richard Elliott Toll, a Pennsylvania personal injury lawyer, churned out phony bills showing that his clients made 1,372 doctor visits instead of the actual 168; the only surprise to fellow lawyers was that he got caught.

Crime in the suites, PI practitioners reply, that's what's really going on in the those self-righteous Big Firms. At Minnesota's largest law firm, Dorsey & Whitney (whose past partners include U.S. Supreme Court Justice Harry A. Blackmun and former Vice President Walter F. Mondale), senior partner James H. O'Hagan was recently charged with swindling clients out of up to $3.5 million as part of an illegal insider trading scheme. He admitted "borrowing" money from client trust accounts, and was disbarred.

And even when it's not technically a crime, the rest of

the profession is convinced there's some pretty shady dealing going on at those Big Firms, and always for megabucks. Looking down on the rest of the profession from their skyscraper offices, Big-Firm lawyers get away with outrageous conduct because everyone assumes their integrity is unquestionable.

Baltimore's blue-chip Venable, Baetjer and Howard, for example, represented Maryland savings and loan associations and also the state agency that regulated them. That might seem to be a fairly obvious conflict of interest, but no one noticed until one of the S and L's went belly up. Then the state of Maryland sued the law firm for malpractice, and Venable responded by calling the suit "irresponsible." But after a little thrashing around, the firm also responded by coughing up $27 million to settle the suit. (They still deny all wrongdoing, which means they can still give speeches about legal ethics at lawyer conventions.)

But even though there may be natural disagreements between PI lawyers and their Big-Firm colleagues, any of them who have experienced marital discord agree on one thing: Those home-wrecking divorce lawyers are the worst.

Shoddy ethics?

Worse than that, divorce lawyers don't even recognize professional courtesy. A highly respected Philadelphia lawyer returned home one day to find that his wife—and all of his worldly goods—had vanished. No warning, no explanation, nothing—until the divorce complaint came.

Still, for sheer numbers, every practitioner knows the criminal defense bar has the most Bad Lawyers. They look the other way while their clients commit new crimes to pay legal fees, in cash, thank you; then they slip some of that cash to the judge. And that happens more than once in a while; when the FBI bugged the Chicago court system in an undercover probe running from 1980 to 1983, they bagged forty-five lawyers on corruption charges.

So lawyers all imagine that Bad Lawyers are practicing

in someone else's specialty, and a survey of the profession, poking into the nooks and crannies, exposing all of the inside tricks and stunts, leads to a startling conclusion:

They are all right.

Bad Lawyers are everywhere.

But a big part of the reason why, as we'll see, involves clients.

Good Guys in Black Hats

Call Bobby.

For years, that's what top mob figures in Philadelphia and Atlantic City have done when they have a problem with the law—call lawyer Robert F. Simone. Like most criminal defense lawyers, Simone's won-lost record would get him fired if he were a football coach, but he has had some spectacular successes, capped by the 1988 acquittal of Atlantic City kingpin Nicodemo "Little Nicky" Scarfo on charges of ordering a rival's murder.

Win or lose, his mob clients have shown extraordinary confidence in him, best illustrated by Scarfo's quip that if he had to have brain surgery, he'd want Bobby Simone to be the surgeon. In short, Simone is clearly part of his clients' world, visiting them in the hospital when they get shot, joining their victory bashes when they get acquitted.

Indeed, one former mob-killer-turned-federal-witness, Nicholas "Nicky Crow" Caramandi, asserted in court that

Simone was literally part of their world, charging that "you've been around these guys so long. . . . They wanted to make you, in fact." Simone immediately shot back, "I'm not a member of the Mafia, right?" and Caramandi conceded he had no knowledge that he was.

But Simone does not deny having had dealings with organized crime beyond simply giving legal advice. A longtime high-rolling gambler, Simone at one point paid loan sharks more regularly than he paid his electric bill. And when he was charged with federal tax evasion, Simone wisecracked, "Who was I supposed to pay, the IRS or the loan sharks? The interest is about the same, the health aspect is a little different."

Two years after the tax charge, Simone was also indicted on federal perjury charges.

By then, anyone who spent any time in Philadelphia courtrooms knew what kind of a lawyer Bobby Simone was.

A Bad Lawyer?

No, an outstanding lawyer.

Intuitive, tough, street-smart, Simone had the rare gift of being able to talk to juries in their own language. With his gunslinger's confidence, it was predictable that he would ignore one of the legal profession's most basic maxims and conduct his own defense on the tax and perjury charges.

He won both cases.

When Robert Chambers was charged with the brutal murder of eighteen-year-old Jennifer Dawn Levin in New York's Central Park in 1986, not many people would have guessed the identity of a central figure for the defense: Jennifer Levin.

She was not present in the courtroom, of course, but defense lawyer Jack T. Litman tried to introduce Jennifer's diary as evidence of her allegedly "kinky and aggressive" sexual appetites. He also filed a legal motion detailing

Chambers's claim that Levin had been the aggressor in a "rough sex" encounter, and made no apology when the motion—filed without any request for confidential treatment—exploded into tabloid headlines.

Observers viewed Litman's defense strategy as indefensible. In addition to the anguish of Jennifer's murder, her family was forced to endure the posthumous trashing of her memory, smeared by the barrage of news accounts of Litman's tactics. It was the sort of lawyer behavior that simply cannot be justified.

Except by other lawyers.

Litman, like Bobby Simone, is viewed by lawyers as a top-notch trial attorney. While his handling of the Chambers case sparked debate among lawyers about whether a vigorous defense can ever be *too* vigorous, no attorney would call Jack Litman a Bad Lawyer. After all, try-the-victim is a tried-and-trusted defense lawyer's gambit; indeed, some legal scholars argue that Litman could have been guilty of malpractice if he had *failed* to use that tactic.

Alice in Wonderland would like that.

The lawyers who appear to be Bad Lawyers are actually good lawyers, but a good lawyer can become a Bad Lawyer by not doing something bad.

This may be a little fuzzy for you, but it's crystal clear to your lawyer. Long before Thanksgiving break, first-year law students have learned that conventional notions of right and wrong, good and bad, are naïve and simplistic. There are always multiple arguments and counterarguments, additional facts to be considered. We're not judges, we're advocates, and when we have a client in trouble, we don't criticize him for his crimes, we try to save his skin.

Why should we do less for misbehaving lawyers?

In short, lawyer training dulls any instinct to make black-and-white judgments about human behavior, and many lawyers in practice spend most of their time—legitimately—defending misbehavior. To get an accurate picture of lawyer misconduct, then, the first step is to agree on a definition of Bad Lawyer that does *not* include lawyers doing what they're supposed to do for disreputable clients.

This is also a prudent way to begin, because the people we're going to call Bad Lawyers mostly make their living by filing lawsuits. No one can prevent that; anyone can sue anyone for anything. As we learned in law school: You can sue the bishop of Boston for bastardy, the question is, Can you collect?

And the answer is that you *can't* collect if what someone says about you is true, so our definition needs to be precise.

What is a Bad Lawyer?

To start, it's not Bobby Simone. Bad habits and unsavory friends are not necessarily inconsistent with first-rate legal skills; and doing controversial things in courtrooms—as Jack Litman did—is what lawyers get paid for. Lawyers in both categories may occasionally step over the line, but this account is not about the Simones and Litmans of the legal profession.

Neither is it about that world-famous lawyer who responded to criticism that he was ambulance-chasing by boasting that ambulances usually chase *him* to disaster sites, not vice vera.

Flashy Mel Belli, "King of Torts," quick with quips, has spent most of his durable career either making or denying eyebrow-raising charges. Anything but retiring in old age, Belli is still blasting away in multifront wars into his eighties, denying his fifth wife's claim that he had beat her and falsely accused her of having affairs with Archbishop Desmond Tutu of South Africa and Zsa Zsa Gabor, fighting an Internal Revenue Service claim that he backdated documents, battling former partners and client malpractice claims.

Throughout his kleig-light career, Belli was often accused of operating at the edge of ethical limits, sometimes over the edge. He offended conventional behavior and regularly antagonized bar association pooh-bahs, all to his apparent delight. Asked his reaction to being expelled from one lawyer organization, Belli deadpanned, "It's about like being drummed out of the Book of the Month Club."

In sum, you might not want your daughter to marry him or like him living next door, but Mel Belli uses the tools of his trade to do what lawyers are supposed to do. He has broken major new ground in personal injury law over a period of decades, defended unpopular clients, and stood up for little people victimized by giant corporations, often with spectacular results.

The definition of Bad Lawyer, then, does not include barristers whose chief faults are flamboyance or shameless self-promotion or both. If it did, all those lawyers who run their mug shots next to the scales of justice in the yellow pages would be on the list.

To keep the numbers manageable, we'll also omit the thousands of lawyers whose basic legal skills are mediocre or worse, and those who, like Philadelphia lawyer Timothy Crawford, Jr., commit incredible blunders. After his client was convicted of first-degree murder, Crawford claimed he just "forgot" to put him on the stand as part of the defense, which would be about like a surgeon forgetting to sew up a patient after removing his appendix. That's indisputably bad lawyering, but our definition is concerned with legal misconduct rather than incompetence.

(Some observers, according to a *Philadelphia Inquirer* account, thought Crawford fabricated his forgetfulness solely to win a new trial for his client, in which case he would qualify as a Bad Lawyer.)

We'll also skip over lawyers who do bad things, but which are not related to lawyering. New York lawyer Joel

B. Steinberg, for example, committed an unspeakably heinous crime and was a practicing lawyer when he did it; Steinberg's torture-killing of his stepdaughter, however, did not seem to have anything to do with his occupation. (After his arrest, though, it was disclosed that New York lawyer disciplinary officials had investigated Steinberg for using cocaine during a trial and for mishandling funds; those charges were dismissed.)

Similarly, Ivan Boesky, inside trader extraordinaire, happened to have a law degree when he fleeced the financial markets for a few hundred million dollars, but he never practiced.

John M. Fedders is—as we like to say, peering seriously over our half-glasses—a closer question. As enforcement boss of the Securities and Exchange Commission, Fedders was a big man in law, business, and at the SEC; at six feet, ten inches, he was a big man generally.

He did not have a happy marriage, however, and when a Maryland judge granted his wife, Charlotte, a divorce in 1985, there was a finding that he was guilty of "excessively vicious conduct" toward her. Fedders admitted violently abusing his wife on seven occasions, and was forced to give up his job at the SEC. But domestic violence occurs in many households, and whatever its origin, it does not seem to be caused by having a law degree. So Fedders would not fit the definition of Bad Lawyer, except for what happened next.

After the divorce, Charlotte wrote a book, *Shattered Dreams,* about the domestic violence in their failed marriage. At this point, if you imagine that Mr. Fedders was ashamed and apologetic, you probably forgot he was a lawyer. Instead of sending flowers, he did what lawyers do: Big John marched into court and demanded a share of the book's proceeds, arguing that the violence was Charlotte's fault since she failed to support him when he was depressed, and anyway, all the publicity had ruined his career. Incredibly, a master in divorce agreed, awarding him 25 percent of the royalties; a Maryland judge reversed that decision a short time later.

Unlike Steinberg and Boesky, John Fedders was never charged with any crime, and as a lawyer in good standing, he would not normally qualify as a Bad Lawyer—except that he seems to deserve a special place in the definition.

To keep it simple, then, Bad Lawyer will mean someone who fits one of the following three groups:

- Lawyers who use their legal training to break the law, or commit crimes in the course of their practice.
- Lawyers who violate any *important* ethical rule of the legal profession. Not surprisingly, there are big rules and little rules and lots of technicalities, so the focus here will be on *significant* professional misconduct, not minor infractions.

  We also need a catchall definition. Some lawyer conduct—like John Fedders's arguing in court for royalties from his wife's book about his violent abuse—is not illegal, not a clear breach of important ethical rules, but it's simply outrageous. To be sure that the definition of Bad Lawyer does not overlook Big John and others like him, the third category is a little more flexible:
- Lawyers who use their legal training to do things they should be ashamed to tell their mothers.

Those are the Bad Lawyers—and as we'll see, their misdeeds are almost always done with malice aforethought.

But something's missing. The legion of lawyers who look the other way to avoid noticing Bad Lawyers should also be part of this picture. After all, lawyers are not jewel thieves; they rarely commit their crimes secretly in the dead of night. Instead, most lawyer crimes—whether bribing a judge or phonying up a personal injury claim—occur during the lawyer's daily practice, which means other attorneys usually know when there's a Bad Lawyer at work.

What definition fits those attorneys who don't do bad things, but also don't report their friends who do?

They could be called the Silent Majority, or perhaps the Unindicted Co-conspirators. But to choose a name like that would obviously be to prejudge the situation, sort of like a judge imposing jail before the defense gets a chance to put on its case.

To be fair, then, the approach here will be to present the evidence, focus on the Bad Lawyers, and then let *you* decide how you would define the rest of our profession.

In surveying the legal profession, a handful of other definitions are also useful. (As you already know if you have ever glanced at your bank loan agreement or apartment lease or any other legalese in your life, definitions do for lawyers what morning coffee does for everyone else; we can't get started without them.)

We've already mentioned the Secret Rules.

Since lawyers are in the business of telling people how to comply with various laws and rules, it's only natural that the profession itself is governed by specific ethical rules. Like everything else in the legal profession, the rules vary from state to state, although they are generally derived from the Rules of Professional Conduct adopted by the American Bar Association. Those rules were most recently revised in 1983, but at this writing, the pre-1983 rules still apply in some states.

The lawyer rules are *not* secret. You could find them at your local library.

But . . . you *won't* find them on the coffee table in your lawyer's reception room, and your lawyer will not offer to show them to you. (Clients cause us enough trouble *without* knowing the professional standards we're supposed to meet.) Your lawyer, if you ask him cold, will probably not know if your state follows the post-1983 ABA rules or the old version. On the off chance that he does, ask him the provisions of any specific rule, such as Rule 1.6 (which has an exception to the attorney-client privilege that permits lawyers to call the cops about crimes their clients plan to commit . . . sometimes) and you're sure to stump the panel.

Indeed, without prior warning, your lawyer might have a tough time putting his hands on a copy of the current rules of professional conduct.

To sum up, clients never get to see them, lawyers almost never look at them and most have no idea what they require, and they are different in each state. Like the laws that the crazed Roman emperor Caligula had engraved on the *tops* of marble columns where no one could read them, our Rules are not technically secret, but they might as well be. Indeed, when I asked for permission to reprint the 1983 ABA Model Rules (which are copyrighted) in this book, the ABA replied to the effect that permission could *not* be granted unless I paid a sum of money—the amount to depend on the nature of the use. (Imagining that this could get very expensive very fast, I dropped the request.)

The various rules of lawyer ethics, then, will be called the Secret Rules.

And even though the ABA did not grant permission to reprint its Rules, a copy of the Rules as adopted in Pennsylvania—which are not subject to copyright protection and are almost identical to the ABA version—is included at the end of this account. But don't flip forward and try to read the Rules yet; without first knowing about the Weasel Words, you might conclude that the Rules are direct and straightforward, meaning what they seem to mean. This would be wrong. In fact, our Rules are designed to pose minimal inconvenience to lawyers trying to make a buck, and as a result, funny things often happen when someone tries to make lawyers obey the Rules we wrote.

Rule 1.5, for example, says, "A lawyer shall not . . .

charge . . . an illegal or clearly excessive fee." Obviously, what's excessive is going to depend on circumstances (and clearly "clearly" is going to make "excessive" more excessive), but just to fix an outside limit, the Rule would probably mean that a fee of, say, $1 million, would be too steep for any firm to charge for a single week of legal work.

Except that, as we'll see, a New York law firm collected a reported $20 million for two weeks' work, and no one seemed to think that broke the Rule.

Why?

Weasel Words.

"Clearly excessive" is a Weasel Word, an ordinary-looking word that is given special meaning in the Rules to balance the ethical objectives against the realities of making a living as a lawyer. Weasel Words cannot make the Secret Rules vanish, but they often do what's next best, which is to make the Rules mean the *opposite* of what they appear to mean.

Once you understand how the Secret Rules actually work and have a little practice spotting the Weasel Words (which are sprinkled liberally throughout), you'll be able to read the Rules like a lawyer.

Another important term to define is Moral Turpitude. It is not a phrase you're going to overhear on the elevator or in the supermarket checkout line, or even at the lawyers-club bar. But it's a term you would hear a lot if you attended lawyer disciplinary board meetings (except you can't, because they're secret) and—remember Paul Mostman, who tried to kill his client?—Moral Turpitude is at the heart of most court cases on attorney discipline.

Simply put, when a Bad Lawyer gets caught, Moral Turpitude is often his ultimate license-preserver—if he can prove he did not have any.

Here's how it works: We recognize that it's generally desirable that lawyers not break the law, bad for appearances if nothing else, but with the benefit of legal training, we also know that's too simplistic. After all, there are serious laws aimed at criminals, and then there are laws about little things that could happen to anyone. So even if a lawyer breaks the law, it wouldn't seem fair for his entire career to be ruined over some minor infraction, for example, adultery or drunk driving, failure to pay taxes, or jaywalking.

But the problem is, how could we say that it's OK for lawyers to break *some* laws?

Obviously, we couldn't—it would be horrible public relations.

So instead, we take a term no one understands, Moral Turpitude, and say that even after a lawyer is convicted of a crime, he can still keep his license to practice, *if* he can prove his offense did *not* involve Moral Turpitude.

Pretty slick, huh?

(The dictionary says "turpitude" means "inherent baseness" or "depravity," and the notion is that some misconduct may involve issues of personal morality but not necessarily have any impact on fitness to practice.)

This may all sound a little vague and confusing, which is the whole idea.

To sum up, since there's no fixed list of which crimes do or don't involve Moral Turpitude, every Bad Lawyer has a fighting chance.

Big Firm is another term with special meaning. The blue-chip Wall Street firms were the original Big Firms, pillars of the profession, breeding grounds for Cabinet officers. Today, Wall Street firms have lots of imitators across the country, so Big Firms include, typically, the largest law firms in any major city, which usually have a corner on the most lucrative corporate work.

But having lots of lawyers does not, by itself, guarantee Big-Firm status; if it did, Joel Hyatt would be a Big Firm, and he's not.

Some cities are too small to have Big Firms, no matter how many lawyers a given firm might have—on the theory that small-town legal work is not sufficiently challenging to justify Big-Firm status. Big-Firm members generally believe they are incomparably better lawyers than their non–Big-Firm brethren (in fact, the opposite is often true), and they prefer to practice only with other Big-Firm lawyers, even on the other side of a transaction.

Big Firms, then, are the legal profession's version of designer labels: They cost a lot more, but they have their own special cachet. To paraphrase the memorable Supreme Court comment on obscenity, we may not be able to define Big Firms precisely, but we recognize one when we see it.

And while it would have been unheard of a few years ago, Bad Lawyers now pop up at Big Firms with increasing frequency.

Finally, we'll sometimes refer to the legal profession as the Club, because that's really what it is. Like a college fraternity or country club, we have intimidating entry barriers, and blackball possibilities, but once a member, fellow members protect their own, so it's nearly impossible to get kicked out. Also, like most clubs, we have our secrets, enough to make a Mason jealous (although not, at least in my experience, any secret handshakes).

These definitions will be helpful in translating a complex subject into understandable terms. But don't get the wrong idea. Just because we've defined Bad Lawyers does *not* mean that we are prepared to concede that they constitute a major problem for the legal profession. As lawyers, however, we are willing to look at the evidence.

The place to start is in the United States Supreme Court, in the year 1883. This may seem to be an improbable starting point on two counts: The high court is usually where stories end, not begin, and the legal profession has undergone dramatic changes in the century since 1883.

Even so, the case of *Ex Parte Wall* offers a handy jumping-off point, because in addition to a lawyer who led a lynch mob, it features a Supreme Court justice who understood the true value of the license to practice law.

"One John, Otherwise Unknown"

If the legal profession is a priesthood, as many practitioners like to imagine, then the United States Supreme Court is our holy of holies.

From the time of its creation by the Constitution, the high court has been a place of potent magic, with power to transform even journeyman judges into revered justices, and ordinary people—even *bad* people—into symbols of precious human rights.

Ernesto Miranda, for example, was a criminal before, and after, the 1966 Supreme Court decision that took his name; he died a decade later in a Phoenix bar, in a knife fight over a card game. *Miranda* v. *Arizona*, however, which requires police to warn suspects of their right to counsel prior to interrogation, still lives, and many officers carry the Miranda warning on a card inside their hats. (Ironically, police found two Miranda warning cards—which Ernesto sometimes autographed and peddled outside courthouses—in his pocket after his death.)

Likewise, on other issues, from slavery to segregated schools to abortion, Court decisions have taken the names of litigants and carved them into historical monuments: *Dred Scott; Brown* v. *Board of Education; Roe* v. *Wade,* in every case a human name, a bitter dispute, a ruling that, right or wrong, changed the lives of millions. Oddly, though, while its decisions regularly provoke furious political debate, the Supreme Court itself remains mysteriously apart from the vortex of political forces that swirl around it, as politicians as savvy as Franklin Roosevelt have learned to their regret.

The other oddity is that the Court retains its special magic among lawyers. We know how our fellow lawyers maneuver and scheme, wheedle and deal, to become judges; and we also have firsthand experience with injudicious judicial conduct. Given that, it might be imagined that practitioners would be cynical about the Court, or at least free from awe.

In fact, the opposite is true. While a relative handful of us will ever argue a case there (or, for that matter, in any other court), every year thousands of lawyers go to the trouble of getting admitted to practice before the United States Supreme Court, just in case.

But if arguing before the United States Supreme Court is every lawyer's dream, then disbarment from practice in the high court itself—which Florida attorney J. B. Wall faced in 1883—is the flip-side nightmare. Any casual observer would have been certain that the justices would be unanimous in their verdict.

The grisly facts were not in dispute.

When District Judge James W. Locke adjourned court for lunch at 1:00 P.M. on March 6, 1882, he saw a prisoner being brought to the adjacent jail by two officers.

When he returned from lunch a little over an hour later, the Supreme Court stated, "the dead body of the same prisoner hung from the limb of a tree directly in front of the court-house door."

The victim was "one John, otherwise unknown."

Approximately two hundred people had witnessed the lynching, but, like a mob hit in a crowded restaurant, no one saw anything.

Furious, Judge Locke pressed for answers, and quickly learned that attorney Wall had been a ringleader. But no one was willing to testify against him, and some eyewitnesses actually left town. Judge Locke finally concluded that local sympathy for the lynch mob and its influential leaders made it futile to try to force witnesses to testify against J. B. Wall. But he ordered a hearing to consider Wall's disbarment.

At the hearing, the only witness was U.S. Marshal Peter A. Williams, plainly as reluctant as the others. Nevertheless, his testimony was chilling:

When I got to the corner I saw the party coming out of the jail with the criminal, the man who was afterwards hanged. They carried him over the steps to the oak tree in front of the steps to the court-house. The crowd gathered around him, and some one threw the man down. . . . I heard the man hollowing. He was put on a dray with a rope around his neck. The dray went off and he fell to the ground about ten feet from a perpendicular; the crowd pulled the rope and he went up.

The marshal also testified that attorney Wall was "one of the party," and that "when going from the jail to the tree, Mr. Wall, I think, had hold of the prisoner; he was beside him."

Judge Locke disbarred J. B. Wall, who promptly appealed to the United States Supreme Court.

To a layperson, the issue would seem fairly straightforward. As an attorney, Wall had taken an oath to uphold the Constitution and to conduct himself "as an attorney and counselor of the court uprightly and according to law." Whatever else that phrase might mean, it seems certain that it would at least mean that a lawyer who dragged a prisoner out to be lynched should be disbarred.

But Mr. Justice Field thought not. He did not say that, of course. Instead, as a well-trained advocate, he emphasized his indignation over the lynching, but found technical and procedural defects in Wall's disbarment.

The majority thought otherwise.

"Of all classes and professions," they stressed, in affirming Wall's disbarment, "the lawyer is most sacredly bound to uphold the laws." Oddly, however, the justices showed more concern for the sensibilities of Judge Locke than for the victim whose last name did not seem important, expressing outrage that the lynching had been perpetrated "in the virtual presence of the court!"

By choosing that particular oak tree, the justices went on, the lynch mob had forced "the Judge of the court, in passing in and out of the place of justice, [to be] insulted by the sight of the dangling corpse."

But whether judicial sympathy is directed toward the lynch victim or the judge insulted by his corpse, how could any justice of the United States Supreme Court possibly argue against disbarment in such a case? As Justice Field explained:

> *To disbar an attorney is to inflict upon him a punishment of the severest character. He is admitted to the bar only after years of study. The profession may be to him the source of great emolument. If possessed of fair learning and ability, he may reasonably expect to receive from his practice an income of several thousand dollars a year. . . . To disbar him having such a practice is equivalent to depriving him of his capital. It would often entail poverty upon himself and destitution upon his family.*

It's a remarkable statement.

In a case that has for its centerpiece a nameless corpse hanging from a tree in front of a federal courthouse, a Supreme Court justice finds disbarment to be "punishment of the severest character" (sort of like lynching?) and inappropriate.

Why?

Because, in simple English, *the license to practice law is worth a lot of money.*

At the time of the Wall decision, of course, the American legal profession did not even resemble today's law business. First, the law was a select calling, with only about seventy thousand attorneys nationwide (less than 10 percent of today's total). That scarcity was not as alarming as it might first seem, however, because lawyers had not yet figured out how to be indispensable in daily life. People started businesses, ended love affairs, served booze to neighbors who ran into trees on the way home, and even managed to deal with death and taxes—all without lawyers.

Out west, a Montana cattle drive that would, when reenacted a century later, require *four* environmental-impact statements, countless releases, permits, insurance policies, and indemnifications, could still, in the late nineteenth century, be run by cowboys, not lawyers. The industrial titans then changing the face of America—building railroads, creating potent industrial monopolies, ushering in the Industrial Revolution—did most of that without benefit of counsel (and indeed, without undue concern for legal niceties).

And attorneys often enjoyed a leisurely pace. Well into the twentieth century, the morning ritual at many law firms started with the opening of the mail; over coffee, the senior partner would pass out the day's correspondence to the other lawyers, making suggestions, commenting on problems.

Attorneys were theoretically subject to supervision by the courts in each state, but in 1882, there was no general code of conduct for lawyers, and it would be another quarter century before the ABA would adopt one.

Put simply, there weren't many lawyers, but also not many laws—and no rules of lawyer conduct.

Not surprisingly, having relatively few laws often meant hard times for lawyers. Many practitioners barely eked out a living, and did not get any respect either, two realities that inspired the formation of the American Bar Association five years prior to the Wall disbarment. The ABA's original purpose was to raise the social and economic status of lawyers.

But while small children were more likely to dream of becoming bad-guy Jesse James or boxer John L. Sullivan than Supreme Court Chief Justice Salmon P. Chase, those who did become lawyers were determined to remain lawyers. If the license to practice did not guarantee prosperity, it was a passport to other areas that often did; the lawyer who obtained the local bank charter, for example, usually became a bank director, and attorneys were often the first to know when a lucrative real estate deal could be made.

More important, the license to practice was—and is—the membership card in a powerful, and wholly unregulated, monopoly. Except for that, though, it would be hard to imagine two occupations having less in common than the nineteenth- and twentieth-century legal professions.

In the century since the Wall decision, the American legal profession has undergone dramatic, fundamental change. First the numbers have exploded, more than doubling between 1970 and 1989. Even though an ABA committee fretted in the mid-twentieth century that "in the face of the country's ever-growing need for lawyers, the law is becoming a dwindling profession," lawyers—like alligators and buffaloes, also marked for possible extinction—have come roaring back in nuisance numbers.

Two thirds of all the lawyers *in the world* are in this country (which makes Bad Lawyers, unlike global warming or pollution, a distinctly American problem). At last count, there were approximately 850,000 of us, roughly 1 for every 400 citizens. That's fifteen times more lawyers per capita than in Japan (a disparity that led humorist Russell Baker to suggest the export of one American attorney to Japan for every Toyota imported).

Well before the year 2000, some new Juris Doctor will have the distinction of becoming America's one millionth attorney—and more likely than not, she will be a woman, if current law school trends hold. And with 75 percent of female lawyers under age forty (compared to 50 percent for males), women will increasingly dominate the legal profession.

A million lawyers sounds like a lot of competition, but there's a catch; in an adversary system, each action taken by a lawyer creates a demand for a second lawyer to respond to it. This automatic multiplier effect is unique to the legal profession. Doctors, in contrast, only make work for other doctors when they make mistakes. But we build business for fellow attorneys whenever we do anything, right or wrong, and as a result, it's unusual to hear about attorneys being squeezed out of business (although the collapse of junk-bond financing has triggered some Big-Firm cutbacks).

Not all lawyers make a lot of money, but since most lawyer prices are—as we'll see—fixed in various ways, those in private practice tend to be comfortable. At the top end of the business, "astronomical" would be a word to describe lawyers' incomes; a 1989 *Forbes* magazine report put the combined annual compensation of 134 of the nation's top-earning lawyers at a cool $860 million.

If the ABA was formed to improve the profession's economic status, it's time to disband it, mission accomplished.

The same fiscal forces that powered this expansion have reshaped the way we practice. While as recently as a decade ago close to half of all lawyers were in solo practice, growing legal complexities make flying solo increasingly perilous, and—as we'll see—lawyers in firms almost always earn more. So lawyers are flocking to firms, and firms are ballooning into megafirms with hundreds of lawyers in far-flung offices around the world.

It has been a head-snapping change. Well into the 1970s, law firm partners traditionally viewed themselves as an intimate, happy band of brothers, working together—and sometimes feuding—like family, all in the same city, professionally linked for life. Today, lawyers are often partners with attorneys they have never even met, in cities they have never visited.

Indeed, lawyers today may have partners who are not even lawyers. Under a controversial new program approved by the District of Columbia, nonlawyers (which will probably mean lobbyists about 99 percent of the time) may become partners in law firms. The ABA rejected a similar proposal a few years before, but it will be back on the agenda, which will force lawyers to face a difficult dilemma:

Should we accept nonlawyer partners (who, especially if they're high-powered lobbyists in places like D.C., might make us a lot of money), or limit law partnerships solely to lawyers, to make certain that we don't lose our power of self-regulation?

(After all, if nonlawyers slip into the Club, maybe the legal profession will no longer be a profession, but just another business subject to outside regulation; there are more than a few bucks riding on this one.)

A prediction: We'll try to grab the money from nonlawyer partners, and fend off the regulators some other way.

The pace of practice has also accelerated sharply. In the old days at Montgomery, McCracken—that is, about twenty years ago—partners would often enjoy a cocktail or two with lunch at the club, as did their colleagues in other large firms. This tended to keep the tempo of afternoon activities civilized. Indeed, upon his return from lunch, one lethargic partner regularly positioned himself strategically behind *The Wall Street Journal*, leaned back in his chair—and took a long afternoon nap. (Occasionally, his longtime secretary would make the mistake of putting through an insistent caller, which invariably drew an outraged roar from behind the *Journal:* "God, can't you see I'm busy!")

How could they do it?

Simple. Except for rare telephone emergencies, the morning mail, dispensed at the ceremonial opening, brought the only new matters that required daily attention. Once that was disposed of, lawyers could ease into the afternoon, and if there was a dropoff in, ah, efficiency, no one noticed.

Today, lawyers are hammered twenty-four hours a day. Legal documents are faxed into law offices around the clock, and morning mail has become an anachronism. Anything important that is not faxed is hand-delivered or sent by an overnight service, and everyone wants instant responses to everything.

Lunch, understandably, is often health food at the desk, and lawyers who regularly drink at lunchtime are about as common as those who take cases for free. Besides the two-martini lunch, another recent legal-profession casualty is the unwritten protocol that gentlemen do not sue each other for legal malpractice. (Indeed, maybe the latter was required to perpetuate the former!) After years of practice on doctors, someone figured out that the same theory works against lawyers. Legal malpractice suits mushroomed—one in seventeen lawyers is charged with malpractice annually, one in six in lawsuit-happy southern California.

All of those lawsuits have driven insurance costs through the roof, one of many items forcing lawyers—who often could not even read a balance sheet, in an earlier era—to concentrate on the bottom line.

In sum, legal traditions that endured for centuries have disappeared in a decade. Quill pens and leather-bound libraries have been replaced by laser printers and computers; leisurely face-to-face meetings between partners are now compressed into brief voice-mail messages. The proud profession has become a busy business, with ethics so suspect that when a lawyer at a real estate settlement recently offered the conventional assurance that a forgotten document would be delivered the next day—"You have my word, as a member of the bar"—even the other lawyers around the table laughed out loud.

And the profession that traditionally frowned on any public advertisement of its services now struts its stuff on TV, as lawyers like Joel Hyatt (". . . and you have my word on it") slug it out for consumer dollars with flaks like Joe Isuzu.

We've come a long way, baby.

Everything has changed. Or, almost everything. We have been careful to preserve one piece of our professional heritage: We didn't change the way we deal with Bad Lawyers.

Why should we?

J. B. Wall got disbarred, the system worked; indeed his case is still regularly cited in attorney discipline decisions today. Critics might want to overhaul the whole system, come up with some high-tech disciplinary machinery for the twenty-first–century legal profession, but that would probably be a mistake.

After all, part of the majesty of the law is its respect for past traditions and practices. We might need to make a couple of minor adjustments, but that's no reason, on the face of it, why our approach to professional discipline shouldn't endure for another century or two.

Keeping tabs on the ethical standards of a million lawyers might be *slightly* more complicated than it was for seventy thousand, but we'll take care of that with computers or something. And the fact that some lawyers today don't even know the *names* of their partners is somewhat troubling, since self-regulation seems to contemplate a profession in which the professionals not only know each other, but something about each other's ethics.

But give us a little time, we'll think of something.

In the meantime, if old attorney Wall were to make a deal with the devil to revisit his old profession, he would find three familiar principles still controlling what happens to Bad Lawyers.

- We make our own rules—and the rules don't automatically kick an attorney out of the Club just because he commits a crime.

  Patrick H. Wright, Jr., and William E. Armstrong, for example, served federal time on extortion charges, and went right back to being Louisiana lawyers in good standing as soon as they got off parole.

  The justification? The Louisiana Supreme Court said that "the character and reputation of each respondent, both before and after conviction, remains virtually intact within their geographic communities."

  Translated from the legalese, that seems to mean that folks don't necessarily think less of their lawyer just because of a little federal felony conviction.

  Even when they get disbarred, attorneys usually don't get embarrassed. Minnesota attorney Tilmer Eugene Thompson evidently did not think murdering his wife for insurance proceeds reflected adversely on his fitness to practice. After serving almost twenty years in the slammer on his first-degree conviction, he came out and petitioned for readmission to the bar. (The Minnesota Supreme Court turned him down.)

- We are judged by fellow lawyers—or lawyers who have become judges—and legal training, as we will see, softens some of those rigid attitudes about right and wrong held by nonlawyers.

  That's the only explanation for the case of Louisiana attorney Maurice D. Robinson, who used client money to build a swimming pool, invest in real estate, and pay his children's private school tuition. If you were the client whose money was used, you might think Robinson should be disbarred—but the court thought otherwise.

  The Louisiana Supreme Court ruled that a three-year

suspension would be punishment enough, noting, according to an *ABA Journal* account of the case, that Robinson "has and continues to give generously of his time and service in behalf of his church."

(Nice for the church, but not too helpful for the old clients.)

- Finally, the lawyers who judge lawyers never lose sight of a central truth, the same one that Mr. Justice Field focused on so tenaciously, namely that *the license to practice law is worth a lot of money*.

Usually that's expressed somewhat delicately, since it's one of those legal principles likely to inflame nonlawyers, but the court in the Wright-Armstrong extortion case above put it bluntly. "Both respondents have suffered imposition of severe penalties," the court noted sympathetically, "in the form of . . . loss of financial security due to confinement and the resultant interruption of their legal practices brought about by the suspension of their licenses to practice law."

Being off in federal prison does tend to interfere with a legal practice (although not in all cases, as we'll see). That was exactly why a Pennsylvania judge sentenced lawyer Anthony Caiazzo, who failed to pay $377,000 in federal taxes, to probation instead of jail time. "In this case I am very hesitant to interfere with your ability to practice law should you be free to do so," federal judge Thomas N. O'Neill, Jr., told Caiazzo, ". . . because that is the means by which you will attempt to make the government whole."

It also beats making license plates.

(This is probably not any sort of preferential treatment; after all, doesn't it seem likely that the judge would have done the same for, say, a cab driver or longshoreman on his way to the Big House for tax cheating?)

But actually, the notion that someone might be allowed to keep practicing law so he can pay fines and penalties he owes for *breaking* the law makes perfect sense—once you master the lessons of law school.

Numquam Dixerunt Legem Nobis Observandam Esse

"They Never Said We Had to Obey the Law"

When giving legal advice to clients, a professor told our class at Harvard Law School, some lawyers make a memo for their files stating the opposite of the advice given.

The *opposite*?

Yes—because the only time you ever need the memo is when the advice turns out to be wrong.

Welcome to law school, where idealistic students learn to think like lawyers.

You could do that without ever going to law school, of course. A drug offender named Gary Presnell learned how to think like a lawyer in Alabama's Maxwell Federal Prison, where he was doing three years, and liked it so much he signed up for three more years of the real thing after his release. His story had a made-for-television happy ending, as he was eventually admitted to the bar by the same judge who had put him behind bars.

A brash New Yorker showed that you could set yourself up as a lawyer the same way you might become King of the Surfers: by having cards printed. His cards identified him as a lawyer named, variously, Peter J. Ford or Peter Horsford, and he handled dozens of criminal cases in Manhattan under both names for several years. Then he was arrested in the New York State Supreme Court, where, appropriately, he was representing a client.

Horsford-Ford was charged with perjury and practicing law without a license. It was not the first time he had been overcome by an irresistible urge to practice law; he was already on probation for impersonating a lawyer.

He had never attended law school.

James Silver, a veteran practitioner, was appointed by a New York court to represent one of the defendants in the sensational Brinks shootout; in another court, he was later charged with practicing law without a license.

Pretenders like Silver, however, represent only a tiny fraction of the non-law school lawyers. Thousands of America's most noted lawyers, from Abraham Lincoln to Clarence Darrow, never saw the inside of a law school lecture hall. In the old days, the way to become a lawyer was to "read" law—which meant serving a rigorous apprenticeship under a practicing lawyer and then passing an examination. It was a mentor/protégé system, and even after the protégé became a lawyer, the mentor remained informally responsible for his professional—and ethical—conduct.

Early this century, however, the American Bar Association launched a campaign to eliminate legal apprenticeships and to require attendance at ABA-approved law schools in their place. The effort was not an instant success; by midcentury, there were still more American lawyers who had been trained by mentors than by law schools. But today, except in a handful of states, legal apprenticeship has gone the way of the traveling snake-oil salesman, both casualties of the professional organizations they threatened, and law school is the only way into the Club.

The reason for making law school mandatory, according to the ABA, was to raise professional standards.

Maybe.

But with law school now spewing out about forty thousand new attorneys annually, quality control is impossible; Bad Lawyers roll into the profession as fast as those lemons come off the line on the holiday hangover shift in Detroit. It could be worse, however, if the way into the Club was still by apprenticeship: How about if forty thousand would-be lawyers all chose their local Barry Denker to serve as mentor?

Ironically, one criticism of law schools is that they are *too* successful, drawing the best and brightest college graduates, attracting "an unusually large proportion of the exceptionally gifted. . . . The net result of these trends," one observer warned, "is a massive diversion of exceptional talent into pursuits that often add little to the growth of the economy, the pursuit of culture, or the enhancement of the human spirit."

The most surprising aspect of that comment was the fact that it was not made by some longtime lawyer-basher or bar association gadfly; rather, it was another shot from that old establishment guerrilla Derek C. Bok, former dean of Harvard Law School.

But while law schools may indeed be guilty of luring bright kids away from careers as philosophers or concert pianists or, at least, ecologists, it's not fair to blame the law schools for the misconduct and abuses of lawyers in practice.

That's because—as we all discover after graduation—what they teach in law school has almost nothing to do with the practice of law.

* * *

"Look to your left. Now look to your right."

The dean pauses, and the students who fill the auditorium wag their heads obediently.

"Three years from now," he continues solemnly, "only one of the three of you will be here."

For generations of law students, that ritual welcome was their first impression of law school, one that was both ominous and accurate. Rigorous, arbitrary, and proud of it, law schools preside over a three-year hazing of pledges to the American legal fraternity that even an Animal House rush chairman would admire. Reading assignments are served up by the pound. Professors grill students endlessly on obscurities that would not qualify for Trivial Pursuit. The competition is cutthroat, grades mostly subjective. And while the traditionally vicious flunk rate has eased, the process still verges on guerrilla warfare.

Students routinely refuse to share notes with classmates who miss a lecture; others deliberately give out disinformation. During final exams, key cases sometimes disappear from library books, neatly razored out. One student in our class who always crammed through the night would slip a blanket under his door around midnight; until we caught on, once we saw his sliver of light vanish we were lulled into thinking the competition had gone to sleep and we could too.

The prize for outstanding performance in law school is an exquisite torture known as the law review, selection for which is an honor given the top 10 percent of the class; the legal equivalent of being top gun. Students on the law review pick some minuscule legal issue, read everything written about it since the beginning of time, then write an article detailing their findings, all on an impossible deadline. The student-written articles, along with others by recognized legal scholars, are published in the various law reviews, which are considered to be the epitome of legal analysis and writing. Translation: They are highly unreadable and do not have pictures.

What law reviews do have is prestige and footnotes: more footnotes than an airline schedule, thousands of microscopic footnotes, so many footnotes that some pages have only a single line of text followed by—you guessed it—footnotes.

Jesse H. Chopper, dean of the University of California Law School at Berkeley, responded testily to an *ABA Journal* inquiry about his law review article, saying, "I didn't write it to set the footnote record." But since he racked up 4,824 footnotes not even trying, you have to wonder how many he might have managed if he had been going for the gold.

Legal scholarship, in short, may be of compelling interest to legal scholars, but it does not normally generate any bidding battles for the movie rights.

Still, for law reviewers and other students alike, law school has its own peculiar intensity, an atmosphere in which abstract and abstruse issues seem vitally important. In many of the best law schools, the intellectual challenge is heightened by use of the Socratic teaching method. That means the professor never actually teaches the students anything by means of a direct, declarative statement (which could come as a jolt to parents struggling to come up with about $20,000 a year for law school tuition). Instead, he simply leads the class through an endless series of questions, on the theory they will gradually discover the truth for themselves.

It might have worked for Socrates, but for most of the rest of us, what we remember is thousands of questions with no answers.

(In contrast, some of the supposedly second-rate schools teach what lawyers actually need to know to practice. One of the best lawyers I know jokes that students in his school were not smart enough for the Socratic method, so they memorized things like "A motion is an application for an order." Fairly basic, but more helpful than Socrates if you need an order from a court.)

What we don't remember, reflecting back on the supercharged law school environment, is any emphasis on legal ethics, which is not surprising, since pre-Watergate, there wasn't any. But the Watergate scandal forced the legal profession to address an embarrassing question. It would have seemed remarkable if two or three leading lawyers in the same firm—or even the same city—were convicted of crimes. How, then, could so many top government lawyers, starting with the attorney general of the United States, be engaged in criminal activity?

What about legal ethics? What were lawyers learning in law school? Stung by criticism, the American Bar Association responded decisively.

It created a committee.

After appropriate lawyerly mulling, the committee treated epidemic lawyer lawlessness by prescribing a small dose of legal ethics—but only for those who had not yet become lawyers. Every law school, the ABA decreed, must require an ethics course in the three-year curriculum.

But there was no recall of pre-Watergate lawyers to fit them out with the new standard ethics equipment, not even a simple consumer alert: WARNING: IF YOUR LAWYER GRADUATED FROM LAW SCHOOL BEFORE 1980, HE/SHE MAY HAVE NO TRAINING IN, OR KNOWLEDGE OF, LEGAL ETHICS.

And of course, a seminar on ethics doesn't guarantee an ethical lawyer. At the University of Southern California Law Center, in a single year twenty-eight students got a slap on the wrist for "fudging" on job resumes. A sympathetic university administrator, suggesting that students felt the pressure of a tight job market, was not overly concerned. "There's been cheating ever since there have been schools," she explained.

Even with the mandatory ethics requirement, it is important to understand that law schools are not generally in the business of teaching would-be lawyers to obey the law.

"I never thought it was the professional responsibility of law schools to teach people not to lie or steal," declared no less an authority than United States Supreme Court Justice Antonin Scalia, speaking to the *ABA Journal*. "That is a public misconception of the role of the law."

There is actually a complicated intellectual debate about this issue (probably started by some of those bright kids who became law professors instead of philosophers), but for present purposes, the important point to remember is that law schools do not usually view it as part of their mission to teach students to obey the law.

If the law school curriculum does not cover either the practicalities of legal practice or the importance of obeying the law, what's the point of law school?

It's a way for the profession to prevent nonlawyers from engaging in the practice of law. Stated differently, law school—and the bar exam—are both basically blackballs, mechanisms to exclude people who might otherwise crash the private Club known as the legal profession. Since what lawyers do is not all that difficult, but very profitable, guarding the gates to the Club has always been a professional priority—as I learned after my first year at Harvard Law School.

That summer, I discovered that the Pennsylvania bar had a requirement that, in order to practice in the state after graduation, one had to be sponsored by a preceptor (an experienced practicing lawyer who would serve as a mentor).

But there was a trick.

You had to pick your preceptor *before starting law school*. Obviously, that limited membership in the Club to those who knew the right kind of people: i.e., lawyers. If, like me, you were not acquainted with lawyers, you probably wouldn't hear about the preceptor requirement until sometime during law school.

By then, it would be too late—you could not turn back the calendar.

But it turned out there was a trick within the trick. I finally found a lawyer willing to be my preceptor, on the condition that his firm would *not*—as was customary—agree to hire me after graduation (they did anyway). My new preceptor simply filed the necessary papers *nunc pro tunc* (literally "now for then"—which is how lawyers ask to be excused for turning in their homework late).

But filing a *nunc pro tunc* application was about like taking a Mississippi literacy test: The outcome depended on the identity of the applicant.

The net result, however, of preceptorship requirements, character references, and other entry barriers to the legal profession was that as recently as 1960, when there were only 209,000 lawyers in the country, 206,000 of them were white, and 202,000 were men.

Those numbers have changed dramatically in the subsequent three decades, of course, but one thing remains the same: Lawyers have a lucrative monopoly, and a central function of law school is to protect it, to make certain that people don't do what lawyers do without joining the Club.

People like Rosemary Furman.

Rosemary Furman was a legal secretary who was good at her job. The Florida Bar Association thought she was so good, in fact, that it went all the way to the United States Supreme Court to put her in jail.

Her crime?

She had not gone to law school. Furman had worked many years for lawyers and judges in Florida, and she had a pretty good idea of what they did every day. She was sure she could do it at least as well.

Whether it's Florida or California or any other state, it isn't complex, is not as exciting as *L.A. Law*, and does not have much to do with the landmark cases we studied in law school.

Except for criminal defense lawyers (less than 10 percent of the attorney population) who in fact argue in court and do things people picture lawyers doing, most of us spend most of our time doing one of four simple tasks.

Revising the form, which means taking the latest will or personal injury complaint or divorce or whatever prepared in the office and asking a secretary to run it through the word processor again, substituting a new client's name and address.

Proofreading. We're expensive proofreaders, but there are two excellent reasons for doing it personally: (1) It's a mindless task that can nevertheless be billed at outrageous hourly rates, and (2) it must be done perfectly.

Otherwise, Sally Jones might receive her will with Nancy Smith named as the testatrix, and she would realize immediately that all her lawyer had done was revise the form—carelessly.

Conducting depositions. Depositions (formal witness interviews prior to trial) are to litigation what cost overruns are to defense contracts.

While there are two basic tasks (one lawyer asks questions and the others listen to questions being asked), all lawyers involved charge by the hour, and most of the testimony has no impact on anything. Not surprisingly, depositions often last a very long time. The task of the nonquestioning lawyers is less challenging than that of a football fan (and attorneys sometimes joke about "sport depositions"), but even at $300 an hour, it is brain-numbing sport.

Talking on the telephone (or dialing-for-dollars). This is the all-time favorite lawyer sport, which is why your lawyer is always on the other line.

In its purest form, dialing-for-dollars is a team exercise, played by small squads of attorneys huddled around speaker phones in different cities, meters whirring profitably away. But even when the call is local, the fact is that lawyers talk mostly to each other, and there's not much legal legerdemain in our conversations.

Rosemary Furman, having watched lawyers practice for years, opened what she called a "secretarial service" in Jacksonville. It was a code that like "escort service," was understood by both her customers and her competition. Not only was Ms. Furman willing to type, she could supply the printed forms people might want typed, and make suggestions about how to fill them out. Her forms covered forty-nine varieties of routine legal action, from adoption to bankruptcy, name change to divorce.

In short, what she did was revise the form.

But she only charged fifty dollars for each form, an uncomplicated fee structure that made her highly popular with her low-income customers and equally unpopular with the high-income Florida Bar Association. Paralegals, of course, do much more complex tasks every day, and like lawyers, they bill clients for their time by the hour. But there is one key distinction: The Secret Rules of the Club dictate that every paralegal must work under the supervision of a lawyer.

Rosemary Furman had gone into business for herself.

And it turned out the Florida Bar Association's view of free-lancers was about as tolerant as that of the Mafia.

They had good reason. It did not take Oliver Wendell Holmes to understand the problem. Good old boys who had scraped through State U realized what would happen if a layperson did for $50 what they charged as much as $150 *per hour* to do.

The Florida Supreme Court appointed a referee to hear charges against Furman, a move that proved embarrassing in itself. Since helping poor people fill out forms did not seem to be a crime in Florida, the only charge that held much promise was the unauthorized practice of law. And that seemed to concede that a legal secretary who could understand how to revise the form might in fact be practicing law.

Undeterred, the referee found her guilty. She was ordered to limit herself to clerical services. She could type information in the blanks, but could not correct errors made by her customers.

"That was a real laugh," she told *The New York Times*. "I had been correcting the mistakes of lawyers and judges all my professional life and now I was told I could not do the same for illiterate people."

So she continued doing it. That put her in contempt of the Florida Supreme Court, which sentenced her to four months in jail. She appealed. The United States Supreme Court delayed sending her to jail, but then declined to hear the case.

Days away from reporting to jail, she finally gave up. She closed her business, sold the building, and the Florida Clemency Board nullified her jail sentence.

While Rosemary Furman's mistake was not attending law school, many who make much larger mistakes nevertheless go on to enter the legal profession. James H. Gilbert, for example, was admitted to practice in Maryland and the District of Columbia, until it was disclosed that he had been indicted for his wife's murder; that charge was later dropped, but a judge in a civil action denied Gilbert's claim to his wife's insurance proceeds, ruling that "the evidence [is] overwhelming that [Gilbert] intentionally caused the death of his wife in order to reap the harvest, namely, the proceeds of these two insurance policies."

Strong language, but the bar examiners were more interested in how Gilbert filled out their forms than in what had happened to his wife, or what kind of person he was. With commendable lawyerly attention to technical detail, they disbarred him for failure to disclose material information on his bar application (he had answered "None" to the question that asked for a listing of all lawsuits in which he was involved).

They did not get excited about the fact, which appears only in a footnote of the court's decision, that while attending law school, Gilbert was a one-man crime wave, being charged with forgery, murder, homicide, and assault. (He was convicted of forgery, and the murder charge was dropped after he pleaded no contest to assault charges.) The footnote concludes: "None of these arrests, convictions or sentences is directly involved in this case," which shows the importance of legal training, since a layperson might have mistakenly thought that a rap sheet of criminal convictions could somehow be relevant to whether Gilbert should be admitted to practice law.

Most states are equally judicious. A few have blanket rules against admitting convicted felons to the bar, but most consider each case on its merits, and in doing so the lawyers who screen new lawyers sometimes demonstrate an uncharacteristic faith in the possibilities for human redemption. The test is whether an applicant has good character, and—incredibly enough—even a murder conviction is not necessarily a permanent disqualification.

The folks who grade bar exams show similar flexibility. Either that, or law students in California (where about 50 percent pass) are twice as dumb as those in Montana (96.7 percent made it in one recent year), and those would-be Washington lawyers (fewer than 50 percent usually pass the D.C. bar) would do better in Oklahoma (over 80 percent). The test givers, of course, all deny that the pass/fail rates have anything to do with how many lawyers a state might have or want, but the fact is that a state-by-state comparison of average rainfall statistics makes more sense than bar exam results.

In a recent year, for example, 85 percent of those who took it passed the Mississippi bar exam. If you stepped across the road into Alabama, you might not even notice it was a different state; folks talk the same, the weather and economy are comparable, football fever is as widespread. But you would certainly notice the difference if you happened to be taking the bar exam, because only 61.2 percent passed.

Some states justify their high bar exam flunk rates with the claim that they are maintaining top professional standards, which might be true if the bar exam actually measured legal ability.

But it does not.

The bar exam is an entry barrier, pure and simple.

"Give me a room full of educated adults five nights a week for four weeks and I could probably get them through the bar exam," Emory Law School dean David Epstein told the *ABA Journal.* "The bar exam is nothing but regurgitation of some very specific information."

Given the strong suspicion that bar examiners rig the results of that regurgitation to protect the lawyer monopoly in each state, it's only natural to wonder whether the examinees play a few games of their own. At first blush, it would seem unlikely; after all, they have just devoted three years of their lives to the study of law, the principles of justice, and the philosophical framework of jurisprudence. After such training, cheating on the bar would be the professional equivalent of treason, the highest crime, something no one would even consider.

In fact, it works the other way.

With the advantage of law school exposure to legal stunts and stratagems, many lawyers-to-be are already expert in figuring out how to get an edge, and present a formidable challenge to test givers. To maintain bar exam integrity, most states now mandate code numbers and photo IDs, and more are considering a requirement that a legal career—like a criminal career—start with fingerprinting.

These safeguards might slow down James Bond, but

they did not stop Gregory James Sanchez, who took the New York bar exam after submitting a forged handwriting specimen and a phony certificate of attendance from Columbia University School of Law. (He was caught and pleaded guilty to felony charges after a Columbia professor got suspicious.)

In California, exam security is so stringent that when a man named Morgan Lamb—who previously had flunked the bar exam—finished a spectacular third out of 7,668, nobody called the cops. But when test officials did their version of an instant replay, someone remembered that Lamb had appeared pregnant. They checked: He wasn't. But she was. It turned out that Morgan Lamb had been a wife in men's clothing; Lamb's spouse, a government lawyer, had worn a mannish hairstyle and button-down dress shirt for the photo ID and taken the exam for her husband.

In Michigan, candidate Lary C. Rand slipped through the security with no problem, but then failed to finish the test. It's not that Rand wasn't prepared—the graduate of Rutgers University Law School in New Jersey had failed the Michigan bar exam on his first try and was determined to succeed this time. But he hadn't counted on being arrested in the middle of the exam on an outstanding New York felony warrant for posing as a licensed attorney.

On the last day of first-year Property class in law school, legendary professor A. James Casner (who was said to have inspired the character Professor Kingsfield in *The Paper Chase* and who, a wit quipped, wanted to change his name to "The" James Casner) startled us by abruptly departing from the assigned material.

Some lawyers-to-be in our class, he predicted with stentorian certainty, would be disbarred or even jailed in the course of our legal careers, for one simple reason: We would mix client monies with our own funds, violating the fundamental prohibition against commingling.

It seemed ludicrous. Everyone in that room planned to be a legendary lawyer, or a millionaire, or a Supreme Court Justice, or maybe all three—certainly no one had given a second's thought to the possibility of ending up in the slammer. Indeed, to that moment, law school training had been so completely abstract and hypothetical that it had not occurred to many of us that lawyers even handled money, much less mishandled it.

Even though Professor Casner had been right about everything else during the year, it turned out that he was only partly right in his prediction. Lawyers do, in fact, often mishandle client cash (although I am not certain whether anyone in our class actually fulfilled the prof's gloomy prophecy). But stealing cash is only one trick in a Bad Lawyer's repertoire, and once in practice, lawyers often discover other temptations that prove even more irresistible.

Lead Us Not into Temptation

This may come as a surprise, but "conscience" is a popular concept among lawyers.

We use it for our clients.

It generally works best when clients need to do something not otherwise permitted by law. If a client wants to welsh on a deal, for example, we'll argue that the agreed-to price is so inadequate that "it shocks the conscience." When a client needs to wiggle out of an ironclad written contract, we'll label the contract "unconscionable" (and therefore unenforceable). There are even some courts nicknamed "courts of conscience," where the judge is supposed to seek equitable justice instead of rigidly applying the law.

Because we throw the word around a lot, the meaning of "conscience" is much discussed in legal literature. *Black's Law Dictionary* (a monster volume popular not for its usefulness in practice, but rather because it's a can't-miss graduation gift for college seniors heading to law school) devotes the better part of a column to various definitions of the concept. But what most of them have in common is that they carve out *exceptions* to legal obligations, instead of giving a guideline as to how lawyers ought to behave.

As a result, none of the technical legal definitions is as useful—especially for a lawyer starting in practice—as the obscure description of conscience in Native American lore.

Conscience, the Indians believed, is a sharp,. three-pointed stone located in the center of your chest cavity. As long as your conduct is moral, the stone does not move, and you don't feel it. When you do something bad, however, your conscience alerts you by rotating, and the points are sharply painful. But if you do bad things regularly over a period of time, the points are gradually worn down until it becomes a smooth, round stone.

When that happens, the rotation of your conscience makes a pleasurable sensation in your chest, and it actually feels good when you do something bad.

As Professor Casner predicted, every lawyer has chances to grab cash from his clients. But beyond that, every new attorney discovers that the practice of law is a fun house of temptations, with fresh opportunities to do bad things popping out every day—and with almost zero chance of getting caught.

Some lawyers resist every temptation. But many others feel, early in their careers, an intense pain in their chest cavities. Because despite the fact that law schools have made legal ethics into a metaphysical abstrusity, every lawyer who had a mother knows, deep down inside—at least the first few times—when something he does is simply wrong.

Let's look at the temptations.

Temptation number 1. Mishandling cash is still the greatest temptation, but commingling is not the most common way lawyers steal it.

The problem with commingling is that, sooner or later, someone almost always notices that the money is missing. For Philadelphia lawyer Jordan L. Peiper, the discovery came later; it was not until 1989 that suspicious relatives found that at least $50,000 had vanished from the widow's trust Peiper had administered since 1973. When Peiper refused to explain where the money went, an angry judge sentenced him to six months in jail for contempt.

But most lawyers who pocket money wrongfully never go to jail because they never get caught.

Why?

Because the money they mishandle is money willingly paid to them by clients for actual legal fees. But there's a trick: In contrast to hotels and car rental companies and dozens of other legitimate businesses, we're willing, actually happy, to be paid in cash. Not all of us insist on it. Joel Hyatt accepts Visa and Master Charge, and Big Firms expect checks in payment of their inch-thick bills. But some lawyers prefer cash so much that they'll discount their fee to get it, and very few attorneys, even in Big Firms or Hyatt Legal Service centers, turn down good old American greenbacks.

Here's what happens when they don't: When a client hands a young lawyer a $500—or $5,000—cash retainer, the lawyer, often for the first time in his life, has a big wad of money, cash money, in his hand. And typically, no one else knows about it, because retainers are paid in one-on-one office meetings, or in a remote corner of a courthouse corridor, or in the parking lot outside the police station.

What should he do with it?

In answering that, the lawyer will find three quick ways to trigger a sharp pain in his midsection.

- He can steal from his partners.

  Attorneys who practice with partners are supposed to put all fees into the partnership pot. The partners will hear about the new client, so the cash obviously must be turned in—but maybe not all of it. Maybe, say, $4,000 of the $5,000 would be enough to turn in. The client will never know and wouldn't care; in fact, some clients don't like the idea of their money being split among partners they've never met; they only want to pay *their* lawyer.

Anyway, in partnerships that handle lots of cash, there's often a suspicion that the other guys are taking a little off the top too. Or sometimes, like Maryland lawyer Herbert S. Ezrin who pleaded guilty to misappropriating more than $210,000 in partnership funds, they steal it right out of the pot.

Even after pleading guilty, though, Ezrin—as a well-trained lawyer—did not see his conduct as black-and-white wrong, but rather, as hazy gray-area behavior.

"Some of my partners allege that I stole that money, and the prosecutor also uses that word," Ezrin complained in a statement quoted in the *ABA Journal*. "I did not steal it. I had kept a record of it, and was prepared to pay it back. . . . I'm not saying I have clean hands, but I feel I have become the scapegoat."

- Lawyers who receive cash fees can also play games on the home front.

  That works several ways. First, by keeping cash secret, the barrister is free to lavish it on the woman (or man!) in his life other than his wife. And even for those faithful lawyers who have not yet discovered loopholes in their wedding vows, holding back a little cash seems to help the household budgeting; the wife can't spend the money she never knows about.

  If there's an ex-wife in the picture (or about to be), that's even more incentive to keep that reportable income at a modest level, so the support payments don't go through the roof. Indeed, lawyers in bloody divorce battles sometimes refer their cases in which clients *don't* pay cash to sympathetic colleagues who do, preferring to get the customary referral fee in quiet cash rather than the full fee in a discoverable check.

A tip for ex-lawyer-spouses: Before you settle up financially, get your ex-spouse's lawyer friends to disclose, *under oath,* their total fees paid to him in the last three years. You—and he—may be in for a surprise.

- Finally, the young lawyer who receives a big cash fee will be tempted to cheat Uncle Sam.

After all, the only way the tax man is going to find out about cash fees is if the lawyer tells him. So guess what?

Occasionally, of course, a tax-evading lawyer will get tripped up, thereby providing a rare glimpse at the numbers involved. In the case of Chicago lawyer Michael J. Guinan, who used phony names, sham corporations, and dozens of bank accounts, there was $300,000 of income that never got reported to the taxman.

Guinan, it should be noted, was not simply another errant attorney. Rather, he qualifies for the top of the heap, one others can look up to, a Bad Lawyer's Bad Lawyer. Already mentioned in this account in connection with the mysterious disappearance of his mistress, he was also convicted of unlawful flight to avoid prosecution, Social Security fraud, and an attempted jailbreak. To top it off, he cut off heirs to his mother's estate by revising her will—after she died.

Tax-evading attorneys are not quite as relaxed as they used to be, because even though lawyers are generally feeling good about the war on drugs, this offensive has created a new complication. The Internal Revenue Service now *requires* lawyers (along with everyone else) who receive a fee in excess of $10,000 *in cash* to report it, and to disclose its source. That would not seem like much of a problem, however, since how often does anyone plop down more than $10,000 *in cash* for anything?

Often enough, it turns out, that the American criminal defense bar is in an uproar, claiming a fundamental violation of attorney-client confidentiality that will make clients unsure whether they can fully trust their lawyer.

"This is just a total government conspiracy to . . . make it easier to convict," D.C. lawyer Allen Dale charged. "They

> try to scare the lawyer by saying, 'We will force you to tell who gave you your fee.' "
>
> So far, that argument has not been a winner, but it certainly stands a better chance than the other one, which is that lawyers shouldn't have to report big cash fees to the IRS because then lawyers will have to pay taxes on them.

Finally, before leaving the temptations of cash, it is worth noting the accomplishment of Philadelphia lawyers Herbert K. Fisher and my old acquaintance Herman Bloom, who managed to get caught up in a cash kickback scheme without even receiving any.

As lawyers for Roofers Union members under a prepaid legal services plan, Fisher and Bloom were paid a fixed fee, *by check*. But when the Roofers Union boss asked for cash to pay off a number of Philadelphia judges, the two lawyers knew where to find some, and they obediently coughed up more than $16,000.

The federal conviction put each of them in the penalty box for a year and a day.

Temptation number 2. We can force our clients to do almost anything, since they are often powerless people in desperate situations.

Like most practical aspects of practice, this does not get a lot of attention in law school. But we quickly discover, as soon as we hang out a shingle, that our relationship with clients is rarely an equal one. Our clients tend to be imprisoned, impoverished, in jeopardy—or all three—which means we hold all the cards.

This has a couple of consequences.

First, since almost every client has some terrible tale of woe, we quickly learn to be unmoved by all of them. Most times, any trace of sympathy or compassion that might be lurking in some remote region of the lawyer's soul vanishes before his law school diploma is framed for hanging.

The teenage drug dealer's grandmother has to use her life savings and meager insurance to come up with the $5,000 legal fee—so what? That's *not our problem,* thank you, *we* didn't do the crime, no one is giving it away this week.

Obviously, that sort of attitude among lawyers might help explain why, when poll respondents are asked to identify the American profession most deserving of respect, only 5 percent pick law. But we're more interested in covering the office rent and buying that new Mercedes than in scoring high in public opinion polls, so don't look for any abrupt shifts in attitude.

The disparity of power between lawyers and clients also has another consequence. Because clients so often encounter lawyers at crisis points in their lives, most of them are not about to question—Lord, lead us not into temptation—whatever the lawyer demands.

Nude photographs of his female client and her daughter were what Indiana lawyer Jack R. Wood demanded, in exchange for his legal services in fighting her mortgage foreclosure. After he got the shots, he had sex with his client as well.

Wood told another client, who was seeking a divorce, that he would give her twenty-five dollars' credit against filing fees if he could photograph her nude. But she told the police, and arrived for the photography session wearing a wire (apparently below the belt, since she let Wood snap away with her shirt off).

Once caught and confronted with his dirty pictures and tapes, Wood asserted that he had been entitled to a Miranda warning before anyone taped his statements. The lawyer, in short, claimed he should have been warned he had the right to a lawyer. He also tried to slide out by saying all of the evidence was subject to the attorney-client privilege. (Sound familiar? That's what the drug lawyers say about reporting who pays their huge cash fees.) But the Supreme Court of Indiana was not buying, and Wood was suspended from practice for at least one year.

As we will see, however, that was not the last of attorney Wood.

Colorado attorney Mark L. Davis also had a client in bad trouble, Mr. C., who needed help in a bankruptcy proceeding but could not afford to pay a legal fee.

Hey, no problem, Davis said he would settle for a Rocky Mountain high. He would not accept cocaine, but agreed to take three ounces of marijuana, giving Mr. C. credit at the rate of eight dollars per ounce against any legal bills.

Davis also got a year off from the law.

Estate lawyers, generally a soft-spoken, solicitous lot (like their colleagues in the death business, funeral directors), would never barter legal work for sex or drugs. But sometimes, codicils to Grandmother's will seem to show her generosity toward the trusted counselor increased in direct relation to her senility, and after she passes on to her reward, heirs are occasionally startled to recognize one of Grandmother's treasured porcelain pieces in the lawyer's display chest.

But that normally happens only when the heirs are not visiting Grandma as faithfully as they should. That's the seed of temptation for the reliable old attorney—whose visits are regular indeed—to make sure he gets some special compensation for enduring all of that senile drivel.

After all, he wasn't even related to her.

Temptation number 3. We get checks with two names on them, and you can't get your share until you agree to ours.

As dirt-poor fourteen-year-old Anthony J. Morris of Mississippi found out, this often ties in to temptation number 2, because the clients who get ripped off most outrageously are usually in no position to question the attorney. Morris was badly injured in a car accident, and, double bad luck, he lived right across the street and a few doors up from the office of attorney Edward B. Moyo.

Moyo took the case.

Within three months, without even filing suit, Moyo managed to get a settlement check for $10,000. Great news for the injured boy, except that Moyo took $9,000 as his legal fee. Then, a second check for $12,500 came in, and after payment of medical bills, the victim's mother recieved the balance in cash: $2,700.

Remember that number.

Because before she had a chance to spend it, Mom was arrested for cashing her deceased husband's retirement checks, and she naturally turned to counselor Moyo.

The bail bondsman needed $200, so Moyo set his fee at . . . guess how much?

$2,500.

When the dust settled, an outraged Mississippi Supreme Court ruled Moyo guilty of "monstrous fee gouging," noting that, out of net proceeds of $17,100, the lawyer had grabbed $9,000 in fees, and also had tried to wheedle a loan out of his client. Attorney Moyo was permanently disbarred, more satisfying than most lawyer disciplinary results, except—as the court noted—it did not do much for Anthony Morris.

"There was perhaps the one chance for Anthony to escape from the poverty of a Jackson, Mississippi, ghetto," the court observed somberly. "It is now gone."

The temptation to muscle his client out of an extra $169,000 also proved too much for Philadelphia lawyer Carl M. Mazzacone to resist. Mazzacone recovered $1.4 million for a pipe fitter deafened in a boiler explosion, then decided his client had not heard their fee agreement correctly. The client thought it was the standard 33 percent; the lawyer said "read my lips," and claimed they had agreed on 45 percent.

The lawyer got the money, because the pipe fitter had

no choice, but Mazzacone also got indicted, since he neglected to pay taxes on the fee. At that point, it was time to cut a deal. Mazzacone pleaded guilty to tax evasion, agreed to repay $70,000 to his client, accepted suspension from practice—and the lawyer who represented the government agreed to *drop* charges that Mazzacone had defrauded his client.

Just a courtesy of the Club; no one thought the client would mind.

Temptation number 4. We hear about things before anyone else does.

At first blush, that's a fairly vague temptation. Plenty of others, from bookies to brokers, headwaiters to reporters, trade in tips all the time, constantly seeking to be first to find new angles. Why should inside information tempt lawyers into trouble?

Because, as New York lawyer Michael David learned the hard way, when you use it to beat the stock market, that's a federal crime. Attorney David was part of the "Yuppie Five," a group of New York professionals who traded on inside financial information. David heard about deals about to be made, companies being bought or sold, then told his fellow yuppies so they could all make a killing in the stocks of the companies in play.

Result: After he was caught, David traded his posh position at Big Firm Paul, Weiss, Rifkind, Wharton & Garrison for the keys to a Manhattan cab, and once convicted, he traded the cab for a federal prison cell.

Temptation number 5. No one is looking.

How honest are you?

"Pretty honest," you might say. But honesty, like virginity, is an all-or-nothing sort of condition, and the only time it *really* gets tested is when no one is looking.

The coffee shop clerk gives you change for a $20 bill

instead of your $10; the harried salesperson misreads the tag on your $79 purchase as $29. The bank machine spews out $1,000 instead of $100. Or like Philadelphian Joey Coyle, you hit the jackpot, and happen to be the only one who sees bags of cash bouncing out of an armored truck.

You can grab a few dollars when no one's looking.

Do you?

Most citizens are confronted with that choice maybe a couple of times in their lives.

Lawyers face it every day.

We routinely handle cash and confidences one-on-one, and because we make our own rules and police our own profession, we have extraordinary latitude. No one knows what we do, so despite our historic fondness for checks and balances, today's legal profession is preoccupied with checks, and concerned mostly with credit balances.

In short, often the only thing preventing a lawyer from acting dishonestly is his conscience—which, as we have seen, is often not nearly as prickly as it used to be.

California lawyer John Patrick Kelly received a check for $34,597.05 to hold in his escrow account after his clients sold their real estate. He felt fine. Stealing $19,597.05 of their money did not seem to cause attorney Kelly any immediate pain either. The lawyer's discomfort occurred only after his clients denied his claim of an oral "loan," and demanded the immediate return of their money.

It was all gone.

Lawyer Kelly was disbarred.

R. Elliott Toll, a Pennsylvania personal injury lawyer, thought no one was looking when he puffed up medical bills by more than $329,000. In fact, postal inspectors were both looking and listening, having persuaded Toll's doctor-partner to wear a wire, and the lawyer received five years in federal prison.

Kentucky lawyer Robert H. Jones fell victim to this temptation, and it was five years before his clients caught on. Until then, everything seemed legitimate. When Jones told a client about the $50,000 cash bail that had been set to free a relative from jail, for example, the client had no reason to be suspicious: As soon as she paid the cash to Jones, the relative was freed.

It was only later that she learned the relative had been released on his own recognizance, no bail required, and Jones had pocketed the money.

That was about the time another Jones client discovered that the $25,000 he had given the lawyer to pay taxes never made it to the IRS, and a couple of dozen other clients faced up to the fact that their lawyer had snatched more than $600,000 of their money—while no one was looking.

Jones probably experienced a sharp pain in his midsection the first time he grabbed client cash (which, according to a *National Law Journal* account, was when $20,000 deposited with him to start a family trust was used to pay office overhead), but by year five, he must have been smiling with pleasure as that smooth stone whirred around inside.

The temptations faced by lawyers, are not—to use a favorite phrase we pick up in law school—mutually exclusive. In other words, just because your lawyer puts the make on you, does not mean he will not also steal your money. Indeed, as Barry Denker demonstrated, when a Bad Lawyer really gets rolling, it's possible to knock off those temptations one, two, three.

Denker gave a client $100 to buy a dress for her twelve-year-old daughter, then persuaded the girl to strip naked in his law office to try on the dress. Charged with corrupting the morals of a minor, he then slipped $10,000 cash to a Philadelphia judge, as an "insurance policy."

Denker was acquitted after a trial behind closed doors, which shows the importance of being adequately insured.

Cash, sex, perjury, bribery—in an age of specialists,

Denker showed that a really Bad Lawyer can still do it all. But while the spectrum of legal misconduct covers an imaginative array of offenses, the motivation for most of it can be summed up in a single word:

Greed.

It's All About Money

Kansas lawyer Paul R. Hess took more than $14,000 from two clients out of the proceeds of their accident settlement, and scraped together as much more cash as he could find. Then he packed up his three children and skipped town. But with his estranged wife in a pursuit that Indiana Jones would have admired, Kansas was not big enough; indeed the continental United States did not offer secure sanctuary.

Hess fled the country but she finally caught up with him in Egypt, where he explained his presence to a reporter by saying he was simply trying to have some "quality time" with the kids. (Back in Kansas, a sympathetic judge agreed that made more sense than jail time, and let him off with three years' probation.)

New York lawyer Barry Grandeau embezzled approximately $1.5 million from dozens of his clients, stealing cash entrusted to him for down payments on homes, trust funds held for college tuition, tax funds due the federal government. He resigned from the bar, was sentenced to one-to-four years in prison, and, according to a *National Law Journal* account, told the court before sentencing:

"Your Honor, I feel terribly sorry for the people whose money I misappropriated. I'm deeply ashamed to be here in this position. I've disgraced the three things I hold most dearly—my family, my profession and the community."

Leslie Ray Smith stole $493,000 from sixteen clients, failed to appear at a New Jersey disciplinary hearing, then dropped out of sight after he was indicted on criminal charges. After years on the lam, he was featured on the nationally syndicated television show, *America's Most Wanted.*

In New York, the law firm of Wachtel, Lipton, Rosen and Katz reportedly came up with a bigger number: $20 million.

But there was no international chase, no criminal charges or prison sentences, no national television features—and, most emphatically, no apology.

It was just a routine legal fee for two week's work.

And firm honcho Marty Lipton told a *Wall Street Journal* reporter that people generally view his firm's fees as "modest" for the services performed, and said that clients who object to a fee can pay whatever they think is fair—but the firm will never represent them again. The firm is able to charge big, round numbers because, as Lipton explained: "We don't have any competitive pressure. Bottom line, we have a superior product."

Lipton's $20-million client was Kraft, Inc., and his firm represented that company in its effort to avoid a takeover by Philip Morris. Kraft, of course, is a big company, and when lawyers get spectacular results for blue-chip clients, they often earn huge fees. Houston lawyer Joseph Dahr Jamail, for example, represented Pennzoil in its monster $10.5-billion wipeout of Texaco, and for that, various accounts put his fee somewhere between $30 million and $600 million. (Jamail declined to narrow that range, telling a reporter his fee was personal, "like your sex life.")

In that context, the Wachtel, Lipton fee would be understandable, except for one small detail:

They lost the case.

Philip Morris took over Kraft.

But the losing lawyers still got a fee that worked out, *The Wall Street Journal* estimated, to an hourly rate of roughly $5,000 per hour for every lawyer on the deal, assuming their meters were running twenty-four hours a day, for the entire two weeks of the engagement.

The moral?

While Bad Lawyers are stealing client money using schemes and scams, fraud and forgery, their take is generally pocket change. The really big bucks go to lawyers with clean hands and larcenous hearts, who have figured out ways to lift up their fees into the stratosphere. Like utility players in the baseball draft, they are *not* necessarily all-star legal talents; even journeyman lawyers can make megabucks. What they do is legal, arguably even ethical under the Secret Rules, and often, it does not even matter whether they win or lose.

In short, Bad Lawyers may be breaking the law, but most of the rest of us have not noticed, because we're too busy trying to break the bank.

Still, lawyers who want to get rich have a problem. (You might think that means about 749,999 problems, one for every lawyer except Ralph Nader, but in fairness, a number of others, from public servants to poverty lawyers, also have higher motives.) It's the same problem faced by plumbers, prostitutes, and all other practitioners who peddle their services on hourly rates.

Simply put, you can't get rich selling your time by the hour.

The problem is twofold: Competition puts a cap on prices, and there are simply not enough hours—everyone is limited to twenty-four each day.

Well, almost everyone.

West Virginia attorney George D. Beter billed West Virginia Public Legal Services for seventy-five hours' work in *one day* of representing indigent clients (billing his travel time separately for each of several clients, even though he made only one trip to one place). The Legal Services director took exception, a West Virginia judge tried to hold *him* in contempt for *not* paying, and a Hatfield-McCoy–style legal brawl ensued.

Most lawyers, of course, do not attack the problem so directly, but all lawyers who charge by the hour and want to make real money have to figure out some way around the normal limits on prices and hours. Oddly, recognition of this fact has come only recently to our profession, but in the few years that we've been thinking hard about money, we've come up with some tricks that would make the Happy Hooker even happier.

Here's a sampler of our favorites.

Leverage. Actually, Xaviera would already be familiar with this. While you can't get rich selling *your* time by the hour, every whorehouse madam and Big-Firm managing partner knows you *can* get rich selling *other people's* time by the hour. In effect, that gives you unlimited hours. The more people you employ, the richer you get. The only secret is to make certain you pay your employees less than you charge your customers for their services. The differential is called leverage.

For centuries, law firms paid their employees (associate lawyers) apprentice wages for their first half-dozen years, promising that it would all be made up to them once they became partners. (Only a mild variation on the old "Work hard for me, young man, and you can have the farm when I'm gone" scam.) It was justified by the notion that young lawyers had not really mastered the revered profession sufficiently to have particular value, and in any case, demand for legal services was notoriously unpredictable.

Since lawyers could not advertise or market their services, no one knew where—or if—the firm would find its next case. Law firms did not have budgets; they simply tried to keep overhead (rent and associate pay) low and hoped for the best. In good years, partners "sliced up the pie" of profits at year's end, and in bad years, they paid cash into the firm to cover deficits.

In 1967, our class started at Philadelphia's Montgomery, McCracken, Walker & Rhoads—a typical Big Firm—at $5,600 per year. We understood that if slicing up the pie left any crumbs, we might also get a year-end bonus of perhaps a couple of hundred dollars.

But that year, the game changed. Wall Street shocked the profession by sharply raising starting associate pay. Big Firms around the country immediately recognized that as a monstrous mistake—and promptly did likewise. Philadelphia firms, including Monty-Mac, jumped to $7,200 (amid widespread partner predictions of doom).

There were two instant results: First, associates woke up and realized that there was nothing in the Constitution or the Ten Commandments or even the Fair Labor Standards Act that said lawyers had to serve slave-wage apprenticeships. It was not a technique to ensure the gradual mastery of a complex profession, we were startled to recognize, but simply a trick to let partners make a lot of money.

That became even more clear once young lawyers started doing the leverage arithmetic. If an associate who was paid $7,200 worked 1,800 billable hours a year at $50-an-hour rates, the firm pocketed a tidy $80,000-plus profit (not counting overhead costs). Perhaps, we whispered in the halls (as the partners had feared we would), old Monty-

Mac could afford even *more* than $7,200. Once that heresy took hold among associates, the revered institution of cut-rate lawyer apprenticeships disappeared faster than doctors making house calls.

But the other consequence was the happy discovery, by partners, that contrary to their gloomy forecasts, leverage could be maintained—indeed, perhaps sweetened—simply by raising hourly rates across the board. Fears that clients might dig in their heels and refuse to pay, or worse, hire in-house lawyers at reasonable salaries and cut off the outside firms, proved greatly exaggerated.

Those two discoveries, along with the 1977 U.S. Supreme Court ruling that lawyers have the right to advertise, have driven Big-Firm economic expansion ever since. Hourly rates are reluctantly raised to cover the now annual increases in starting associate pay, and if those greedy associates demand more next year, we'll be forced to jack up rates again.

How high can it go?

Only a few years ago, $50,000 seemed like a natural cap for first-year attorney pay, and with starting salaries now somewhere in the $80,000s, some observers today think $100,000 is the ultimate upper limit. But since those salaries have nothing to do with legal skill or experience, the real answer is that the only actual limit on Big-Firm salaries—and charges—is what the market will bear. So far, rates of $200 an hour for routine work have gone down without a whimper, and $400-per-hour charges are not uncommon.

Somewhere along the way, partners realized they could do more than simply hope for the best at year-end pie-cutting time. They could replace that faithful senior secretary who typically served as law office manager with a gimlet-eyed, numbers-crunching, M.B.A.-wielding financial director. Then they could set a budget, back it up with a slick marketing program, chase the receivables, and cut out dead wood (much of which, in a kinder, earlier era, would have been referred to as "our beloved senior partner").

They could, in short, run the place *like a business.*

In the beginning, that was controversial. Peter Megargee Brown, a highly respected New York practitioner, delivered a widely acclaimed speech before the American Bar Association in 1985 in which he bemoaned the "shortsighted attitudes and perspectives of a large number of American lawyers that practice law as a business rather than as a profession." Many others have expressed similar sentiments.

But back in the accounting departments of the big Wall Street firms, no one paid too much attention, because they had stumbled onto one profound distinction between the legal business and every other business in America. Instead of projecting how many Chevys or dishwashers or widgets the public will buy next year, then figuring out how much it will cost to manufacture them, and hoping to keep close enough to projections to make a reasonable profit, *they could do it the other way around:*

The partners could *start* by deciding how much money they would like to make. Then, compute how many billable hours they need at what hourly rates to hit that target, set the rates at that number, and then simply require their associates to work that number of hours.

At present, for example, Big-Firm associates are typically *required* to bill 2,000 hours a year, and Wall Street, having invented the game, is pushing up to 2,500 and even beyond.

(Associate pay may be cushy, but, as I learned during a corporate transaction with a New York firm, there's no time to smell the roses, even if there happen to be some in those ornate vases in the reception area. After we broke off our negotiation at about 4:00 A.M., I dragged myself back to the conference room at 7:00 A.M. to start again, and was startled to find that the New York associate had *not* grabbed a catnap. Instead, he had been at his desk from 4:00 until 7:00—working on another deal. Standard operating procedure, he said, adding that he rarely went home in the evening during the week, and often worked through the weekend as well.

(Maybe the old apprenticeship—which usually involved about 1,600 billable hours a year—was not so bad after all.)

In short, the explosion of Wall Street legal charges, which, rather than trickling down, gush through Big-Firm imitators across the country at whatever levels lawyers think the market will bear, have nothing to do with the complexity of legal work or the cost of doing it. It has everything to do with the eye-popping discovery that, by raising both hourly rates and total required billable hours of associates, partners could jack up the leverage to earn as much as they choose—at least in New York.

There, in the largest firms, that number currently works out to *average* annual compensation in excess of $700,000 for each Big-Firm partner.

But that's New York. Elsewhere, times are much leaner. At the biggest East Coast firms outside New York, for example, average partner income is only around $250,000.

You might wonder about competition, but among Big Firms, the only competition is for clients. And because Big Firms have successfully peddled the myth that much of the most lucrative corporate legal work can be performed competently *only* by Big Firms, clients do not have a lot of choices. No one cuts prices and every Big Firm in a given city pays associates the same.

But when you think about that, it makes sense. What would be the point of being in an unregulated monopoly if you had to grub around with price competition?

Still, this sometimes comes as a shock to new attorneys who have not yet learned to think like lawyers. Indeed, third-year law students who have just completed antitrust courses are regularly startled when they interview with Big Firms and ask what the starting pay will be. The standard answer is, "We'll pay whatever the going rate is in our city."

That would lead you to conclude that starting lawyer pay must be set by the mayor, or by God, or by astrologers or someone, since lawyers seem to have nothing to do with it, but whoever sets it, the starting salary is the same at every Big Firm in the same city.

Percentage fees are another trick lawyers use to get past the limits of hourly rates. Plaintiff lawyers have known for a long time that it's worth taking the risk of getting no fee when you lose if you get a fixed percentage of the recovery when you win. Thirty-three to 40 percent is where the figure is usually fixed, so when Kansas lawyer Gerald Michaud won a $16-million verdict against Playtex International for toxic shock syndrome, his $4-million fee was actually modest.

In total, according to a *Forbes* magazine survey, plaintiff attorney contingent fees exceed $10 *billion* a year. You might imagine that that number has something to do with your insurance premiums going through the roof, but any decent plaintiff lawyer can explain—with a straight face—why you should be grateful for the legal services they perform.

Big-time plaintiff lawyers are almost never in Big Firms (which are typically defense-oriented), and while the Secret Rules offer no obstacle to Big Firms charging percentage fees, they have been uncharacteristically bashful about doing it. Wachtel, Lipton, which does charge a percentage of the total dollars in a deal, is a standout exception, along with most of the lawyers in the entertainment industry. And while some firms will charge a "success factor'' premium (carefully calculated to be the largest number the client might pay without squawking) for a good result, most Big Firms stick with the trick that made them big, hourly rates.

But before you send off a charity check to your favorite Big-Firm lawyer, you should know about the trick of *Running the Meter,* which Big Firms do as shamelessly as any Manhattan cabbie. In brief, it translates into excessive numbers of lawyers devoting endless hours to a legal project, without producing any concrete legal benefit for the client. The corporate securities law practice, which produces those prospectuses that list dozens of reasons why no sane person would buy the stock described in the booklet, sometimes elevates this to an art form.

During the drafting of one such prospectus, after long days of work, with a team of lawyers arguing over shades of meaning, moving commas around and then moving them back, haggling about type styles and format, the client appeared and asked the status. On being told that a great deal more drafting would be required, the client—who happened to have a law degree and understood the business—exploded. ''You're just running the meter here, and that's fine,'' he snapped. ''I understand that it's a public offering, so you're going to come in with a legal bill around a hundred thousand dollars—because that's what the bill always is, in a transaction this size. I accept that, I'm happy to pay it.

''But for God's sake,'' he finished, ''don't sit here and pretend you're doing anything useful, just clear out of my conference room and send me a bill for your normal fifteen-hour day!''

But don't prejudge.

No one should be critical of Big-Firm lawyers for running the meter that way, because it's so much a part of the practice that most of them don't even realize they're doing it. Or, as a prosecutor would say, they lack criminal intent.

Instead of running the meter, some lawyers create billable hours the old-fashioned way: They simply make them up. Given the opacity of the average legal work product, what client can say if it should have taken twenty hours or thirty-five?

(An ancient lawyer joke has Saint Peter verifying his records on a newly arrived attorney, noting that the man's age was eighty-seven when he died. The lawyer says that's incorrect, he actually died in an accident at age fifty-six. Saint Peter: "Oh, I was working from your billing records.")

Minimum billing units are used by many firms to avoid the administrative nightmare of keeping track of thirty-second phone calls and two-minute conferences. That can mean that whenever lawyers do *anything* on a client matter, even if it takes five seconds, the bill will reflect the minimum unit, often 20 percent of an hour, or twelve minutes.

With the benefit of law school training, it does not take most lawyers long to figure out that if they dictate twenty quick one-sentence letters first thing each morning, they're already up on the board with four fast billable hours. And if they happen to receive answers to those letters a few days later, the time spent reading them is a bonus.

Cost recovery is another trick.

For most of our profession's history, believe it or not, lawyers have been ripped off by greedy clients. Yes, they paid our hourly rates, and yes, we got a fat chunk off the top of their personal injury recoveries, but they stuck us with charges for items like telephone calls and document copies. We were slow to see how much that cost us, because until a few years ago, even lawyers had the foolish idea that a client who paid, say, $200 an hour for legal services might think that somehow covered the lawyer's overhead.

Wrong.

Wall Street figured this one out too, and as a result,

we now know that clients should pay such charges. They're simply included as another item on the bill. And if the number on the bill seems to be higher than what you would expect to pay (say, fifty cents a page for photocopying instead of the five or ten cents you might pay at the local Mister Copy), that's because the law firm had to make a big capital expenditure to buy the copy machine in the first place.

That's only fair.

There wouldn't have been any need to buy the machine if you hadn't kept pestering us for copies of the documents in your case. But since you did, we had to figure out how to avoid getting wiped out on big-ticket items like copiers, and it turns out that our little per-page premium adds up to a tidy big sum.

How much?

A lot, because, while legal expertise may be what we sell, paper is our most important product.

If Midas had stumbled onto this trick, he might have quit worrying about gold.

It's all called cost recovery.

And we're always on the lookout for more costs to recover. Those magazines in our reception areas, for example, are only there for clients to read, we never look at them, and if you add up the total subscription costs, its not a trivial number, so maybe . . .

Rule 1.5 of the Secret Rules, as adopted in a number of states, says that a lawyer shall not charge a "clearly excessive" fee. If the fee is just plain excessive, that's okay; what we're trying to stamp out here are the *clearly* excessive fees.

But that's not as easy as it sounds. To help lawyers figure out when a huge fee spills over from excessive into being clearly excessive, the Rule specifies a number of factors to consider. At first glance, most of them look pretty reasonable: the time and skill required, the novelty of the question, the amount involved, the results obtained, the experience and reputation of the lawyer.

In practice, however, those are actually Weasel Words, which effectively gut the Rule.

Here's how it works: Wachtel, Lipton gets a reported $20-million fee for two weeks' work. Clearly excessive? If you think so, you're obviously not a lawyer and you also haven't been paying close attention.

The legal effort only took two weeks, but lawyers will agree that it required great technical skill. The question may not have been novel, but the amount involved was $12.9 billion, the price Philip Morris ultimately paid for Kraft, and Lipton claimed his work had produced an additional $2 *billion* for Kraft shareholders (even if the company did get gobbled up). The clincher: Marty Lipton unquestionably has a premier reputation and vast experience in the takeover field.

Result: a $20 million fee would seem to be fine, thank you, under the Rule.

And for those rare occasions when a legal fee is clearly excessive despite all the Weasel-Word loopholes, the Rule has one more escape hatch for greedy lawyers. It allows them to consider the fee "customarily charged in the locality for similar legal services."

Translation: If lawyers in those parts have gotten away with jackpot fees in the past, it's okay to keep doing it.

Despite a stern-sounding Rule, then, the legal profession's limits on fees boil down to exactly what you would expect from a monopoly that makes its own rules: *There are no limits on legal fees.*

If big money is moving around, lawyers are going to snag as large a chunk of change as they can.

But don't misunderstand that. We're also happy to get big fees when there's *not* big money moving around, as when three Iowa lawyers submitted a fee bill for $96,422.49

in a case where the plaintiff's verdict was only $1,500. The court later reduced that fee. But another Iowa court approved a $21,508 legal fee in a civil rights case that must be the granddaddy of them all, since the amount of plaintiff's verdict was $1.

There are occasional spoilsports who grouse about legal fees, but what they generally have in common is that they're not getting any. Supreme Court Justice Harry A. Blackmun (who pulls down $110,000, about the same as a kid three years out of law school on Wall Street), dissented from a fee award of $69,661 to a lawyer who had been court-appointed as a special master, saying: "It is difficult for me to accept the fact that in Denver, Colorado, this partner's time is now worth $290 an hour, having been increased from $265. . . .

"It seems to me," Blackmun continued, "that 'establishment' law firms are doing themselves and the public a disservice by asserting fees of this magnitude so persistently over dissents from the court."

Big Firms noted that respectfully, but none of them rolled back their rates.

Not all lawyers, it should be added, are rich or about to be. An *ABA Journal* study in 1988 put the *median* income for lawyers across the country at $68,922, which means, as the *Journal* noted, that "more than half the nation's lawyers earn less than the starting New York associate."

For veteran practitioners, such as Minnesota lawyer John J. Flanagan, that's pretty humiliating, so Flanagan decided to supplement his income. After more than twenty-five years in practice, according to a *National Law Journal* account, he began to avoid his clients, then vanished. Chased by local police, the FBI, IRS, and Customs agents, he was finally captured in Utah, and charged with stealing as much as $1 million in client funds.

He landed in jail.

That seemed like a tragic result, particularly since it was probably unnecessary. If Flanagan was desperate for money, he might have been able to get plenty of it, all cash and all legal, simply by moving into a new area of practice: Drug law.

Feeling Good

There's a lawyer shortage.

What?

Even though we've been reproducing like rabbits for the last couple decades, there are still not enough—specifically, criminal defense lawyers. Fewer than 10 percent of the nation's 850,000 attorneys are following in the footsteps of Perry Mason and F. Lee Bailey, and some defendants remain in jail because they simply can't find lawyers.

If you find this scarcity amid plenty to be puzzling, you've forgotten what we just learned: It's all about money. Or at least mostly about money; it also has to do with lawyers feeling good, which, this once, involves something other than money.

But let's start with the money part.

Here's the problem: With a few notorious exceptions such as Leona Helmsley, rich people do not ordinarily wind up on the receiving end of criminal charges. Even when they do, like Leona, they usually favor the discreet sort of crimes engineered by lawyers and accountants, so they don't get caught all that often.

The people who commit crimes and get caught, then, are usually poor people, and that's our basic dilemma: How can a poor person charged with a crime pay enough to make a criminal defense lawyer rich?

Needless to say, we've figured out a few angles on this, so it's not as hopeless as it first appears. Kentucky lawyer Robert Jones worked the most obvious one: Relatives of criminal defendants sometimes have money (at least until they meet the criminal defense lawyer) that they're willing to spend for the family honor. Close friends, especially girl friends, will sometimes ante up for the attorney (although being tossed in the slammer sharply reduces the list of friends that you consider close).

Some defendants, even poor ones, have assets that can be converted to cash: perhaps a car, occasionally some home equity, more likely a stash of drugs or gold chains from previous crimes. Once in a long while, a loyal employer will offer financial support for the accused. And maybe once or twice in a lawyer's career, he'll hit the jackpot with a Charlie Manson or even a colleague like Joel Steinberg, criminals whose deeds are so lurid that the lucky lawyer can get paid from book and movie proceeds (in states that don't have a rule against that).

Much more often, however, while the lawyer looks the other way, criminal defendants come up with money for the lawyer by doing the obvious, another crime.

(Bad Lawyers don't have a monopoly on this payment plan; crooked judges use it too. During his federal extortion trial, in which he was convicted of fixing fourteen cases, Judge Kenneth Harris of Philadelphia was accused of once suggesting that a shoplifting defendant steal the money to pay him off.)

But even when one of those grubby gambits works out,

criminal defense lawyers live with gnawing knowledge that each new case is going to bring a new problem in getting paid. As the years roll by, that encourages lots of them to look for other specialties.

That's the major reason why criminal defense lawyers may be an endangered species.

There are also a couple of other explanations. Representing scumbags (as lawyers often affectionately refer to their criminal clients) is not nearly as fulfilling in real life as on TV. They constantly lie; even when they *can* pay a fee, we have to get every penny up front or we'll never see it; they're always looking for ways to screw everyone, starting with the mouthpiece; they never show up on time for appointments; and as companions they are, generally, scumbags.

The other problem with criminal defense, I discovered early, is that you can lose even when you win. Based on an evidentiary technicality, I once beat the rap for a young criminal who had, he and I both knew, committed a brutal assault on a milk truck driver. He had a long prior record, which made my performance even more satisfying.

Except that I kept remembering he almost killed the truck driver, and had committed other violent crimes before, and was now back on the street—thanks to me.

Sure, I had studied the great constitutional decisions that guarantee every defendant's right to counsel, and fully believed Sir William Blackstone's majestic maxim, "It is better that ten guilty persons escape than one innocent suffer." The government's obligation to prove every criminal charge beyond a reasonable doubt, using lawfully obtained evidence, is unquestionably a cornerstone of American freedom, and any lawyer who frees a client on a constitutional technicality can take pride in having helped preserve that freedom.

But even enshrouded in all that constitutional majesty, *it just didn't feel good* to have put the criminal back on the street.

Moreover, even if criminal clients paid legal bills, told the truth, and weren't scumbags, something like 90 percent of them get convicted, which means there's no joy in the defense lawyer's won-lost stats. And even when we win, we often know the defendant really did it, and there's not much pleasure in that either.

But wait.

Don't retire.

Don't chuck it all and take up personal injury.

Would you stay in criminal defense if there was a specialty where you could make top dollar on every case, all cash money, with six-figure fees being routine?

No?

How about if your clients, instead of being scumbags, were important citizens in the international community, "very high-class people," as one lawyer put it, even, sometimes, heads of state?

Still no?

Then what if you didn't have to worry about the social implications of winning, because you knew that even when your criminal clients made it back to the streets, millions of respectable citizens were doing the same things as your clients?

Now that, many lawyers have concluded, would be a legal specialty too good to turn down.

Welcome to the war on drugs, where battalions of lawyers are enlisting with the bad guys.

It's a war that is pumping new life—and cash—into the slumping criminal defense business. Drug lawyers have discovered they can get rich and feel good about it at the same time. The war may be against drugs, but what the drug lawyers are defending is the good old Constitution, which is why a lawyer like Miami's "Diamond Joel" Hirschhorn can pose proudly for a *Newsweek* shot aboard his forty-foot cabin cruiser, the *A Quit-All* (a little precious, Joel?), and call it "the boat that drugs bought."

San Diego lawyer Francisco Alatorre felt righteous

enough about his work to come roaring back after the Drug Enforcement Administration seized $1.8 million of his *cash,* along with other assets, and linked his Mexican clients to the assassination of a DEA agent. Alatorre slapped a $46-million defamation suit against DEA, claiming the feds were interfering with his client relationships.

If Alatorre is right, though, and DEA chases his drug clients away, the one certainty is that they will not lack for legal representation. Lawyers everywhere are trying to muscle into drug defense work, snapping up those narco-dollars like bluefish in a feeding frenzy. The *National Law Journal* reports that one Miami lawyer even advertised in the drug magazine, *High Times,* with the slogan "Give Your Bust a Lift."

Good times, but drug lawyers know they need to get that cash quick, because good times may not last.

As we'll see, there's already an ominous cloud on the horizon.

But not all lawyers have noticed it, because in addition to defending drug dealers, lots of them are out there in the trenches with their clients—doing drugs. That, apparently, can feel good too.

Roger M. Simon, for example, discovered in drugs an exciting alternative to all of that boring legal paperwork. "I did it [drugs] because of the intrigue," Simon said, during his disciplinary proceeding. "I did it for the escape. I did it to see if I had the guts to do something that was inherently dangerous."

He did and it was.

Jailed for his role in a cocaine deal, Simon was then disbarred by the Pennsylvania Supreme Court, which rejected his explanation that his judgment had been clouded by his wife's loss of her job and his former partner's theft from an escrow account.

But whether as advocates or addicts, American lawyers are deeply involved in the drug war, and whatever the ultimate outcome, the legal profession has already taken major casualties.

Looking back, it seems almost inevitable that the two giant unregulated monopolies, the drug cartel and the law cartel, would get together. Indeed, if an investment banker had been engaged to analyze the two industries for megamerger possibilities, the report would have been succinct: a perfect fit.

To begin with, the sizes are right, market positions similar. Drugs and law are both robust, multibillion-dollar growth industries that have been around a long time, but really came into their own only in the last two decades. Both market their products at the retail level; they understand that marketplace. And astonishingly, considering the juggernaut revenues of the two industries, they are both one hundred percent privately owned, no problems with the SEC.

But the real sizzle in the deal is the mesh of corporate cultures. The organizing principle of the drug business is secrecy; the legal profession is a labyrinth of laws and rules that not only *require* lawyers to keep secrets, but give special protection to secrets concerning illegal activity.

To top it off, the drug industry churns out oceans of money, all cash; lawyers, as we have seen, are often fixated on money, with a widespread weakness for cash.

One more thing.

No one had to sell the deal to the drug bosses, because they need lawyers whether they like them or not. But given the urgent national priority of the drug war, there might have been spotty resistance in the legal profession to the idea of fighting with the wrong side—except for the Constitution.

That's what makes us feel good, as advocates. The lawyer's duty is right there, spelled out in the United States Constitution. "In all criminal prosecutions," the Sixth

Amendment states, "the accused shall enjoy the right . . . to have the assistance of counsel for his defense."

For most drug lawyers, that's the beginning and end of the discussion. Since drug dealers are not exempted from the constitutional guarantee, the counsel who assist them start out on the moral high ground.

But the terrain turns swampy pretty fast. With all that cocaine cash splashing around, the list of tasks lawyers might do to provide "assistance of counsel" has become fairly imaginative. And the problem is not limited to sleazy fringe lawyers desperately scrounging for fees, as Harvard Law School graduate Anthony C. Castelbuono demonstrated in New York.

Once he got into the drug scene, Castelbuono slipped into the laundering business, taking small-denomination drug money to Atlantic City casinos, where he exchanged them for larger bills. Then, he smuggled those out of the country into Swiss bank accounts.

"I was a success at everything except as a criminal where I was a complete failure," he told the judge at sentencing, shortly before His Honor handed down a fifteen-year change of address, from Manhattan's Waterside Plaza to federal prison.

Actually, though, if the Harvard lawyer had done his homework, he would have realized he was being a little hard on himself. The average convenience store heist nets only $446, according to the U.S. Department of Justice Bureau of Justice Statistics and even professional bank robbers grab, on average, only $3,048 per job. So Castelbuono was not a *complete* failure as a criminal, since he managed to launder a cool $3 million before he got caught.

Out in Iowa, far from the evil temptations of Gotham, Joseph E. Owens also found out how fast the high ground can turn squishy. When attorney Owens pondered the Sixth Amendment, his idea of "assistance of counsel" included collecting debts for one of his clients who was, unfortunately, in prison.

The client had sold disposable merchandise to Lisa and Rusty Bowen on credit, not as risky as it sounds, since he took title to their car as collateral. After he was locked up, he asked attorney Owens to collect his collateralized debt, which probably did not set off any alarms, since that's something lawyers do every day.

The only problem was the merchandise, which was cocaine. The lawyer made a house call, asking for the coke back or $1,000, and Lisa—wearing a wire—gave him the grand in exchange for the return of the car title.

Convicted on felony charges, Owens received a mild ninety-day jail term, and the Iowa disciplinary board recommended a comparably soft eighteen-month suspension from practice. But the Iowa Supreme Court yanked his license, saying: "We do not think a lawyer who had a part in a conspiracy concerning illegal drug traffic possesses the qualities of good character essential in a member of the Iowa bar."

Not all states, as we'll see, are so finicky.

Still, even in the face of harsh rulings like the Iowa Supreme Court's, American lawyers remain steadfastly committed to their constitutional duties under the Sixth Amendment. Despite career risks, hordes of lawyers stand ready to render assistance of counsel, even to highly unpopular figures like Medellin cartel boss Carlos Lehder.

Probably many lawyers would have taken his case *pro bono,* even if Lehder could not have afforded the $2.5-million legal fee he reportedly paid.

Oddly, though, with all of the lawyer enthusiasm for protecting constitutional rights in the drug business, one group of citizens has been firmly shut out: informants.

"I find them [informants] sleazy, morally deficient people," Miami drug lawyer Irwin Lichter told *Newsweek* (an interesting lawyer description of witnesses who tell the truth under oath). Lichter added that "snitch attorneys" might have trouble finding work, an observation reinforced at a Florida seminar for drug defense lawyers, where one of the topics was "The Care and Feeding of Rats."

But informants aside, what varieties of assistance does counsel offer, to protect the constitutional rights of citizens wrongfully charged with dealing drugs?

- They form corporations, a basic lawyer task, the only surprise being that, after formation, the corporations never have any business or meetings, since their only function is to launder drug money.

  But how could the lawyer know that?

- Lawyers help their clients locate scarce raw materials. We've been doing that for centuries, so Philadelphia lawyer Barton Pasternak probably thought it was part of his job. Anyway, how could any liberal-arts-trained lawyer (who maybe flunked high school chemistry) be expected to know that phenyl-2-propanone, or P2P, is the critical chemical needed to make illegal methamphetamines?

  A federal court, however, skimmed right over those explanations, and handed Pasternak three years in prison and a $75,000 fine, for conspiring to distribute P2P.

- Two New York lawyers assisted their client by investing $16,000 in a cocaine deal, a Philadelphia lawyer helped his clients by trying to bribe a witness, and many lawyers are willing to do their part by accepting drugs instead of cash in payment of legal fees.

- New Jersey lawyer Gerald M. Goldberg assisted his client much more innocently, by simply lending him his driver's license so the client could check books out of the library. How could Goldberg know his client was studying how to make drugs instead of, say, boning up on the classics?

  Helping someone use a library, of course, is not a crime, but obtaining phony identification to set up a Swiss drug-money-laundering scheme is, and Goldberg did that too.

> At sentencing, the lawyer said, "I foolishly closed my eyes to what I was doing," which was a blatant lie, since he had made $3.5 million by distributing *nine tons* of P2P over a three-year period, hard to do that with your eyes shut.
>
> Still, he walked away with a mild $5,000 fine and three years' probation, illustrating that crime pays very nicely, thank you.

In fairness, though, it should be noted that not all drug lawyers are in cahoots with their clients. In fact, in a bizarre pattern reversal, one Philadelphia lawyer was accused of the opposite. Testifying in a police corruption trial, a former narcotics squad cop said that he found a brick of cocaine and a trash bag full of marijuana in a drug dealer's apartment—after getting a tip from the dealer's attorney.

The officer assumed the lawyer was simply trying to stir up some legal work.

The lawyer denied it.

Whatever the facts, the denial was probably prudent, because the drug scene is no more hospitable to lawyer-snitches than to any other informants. Consider: Under investigation for laundering drug money, Beverly Hills lawyer Nathan Markowitz was gunned down in an L.A. parking lot. No one actually said the killing was to keep him from talking, but police were able to rule out robbery as a motive.

That's because the shooter left the lawyer's walking-around money untouched in his pocket, and that was $56,000, cash.

Martin Light had a schedule conflict.

The Brooklyn criminal defense lawyer was supposed to be in a Manhattan courtroom representing a client accused of heroin trafficking, at the same time that he was due in a Brooklyn courtroom, where the defendant was also charged with possession of a huge quantity of heroin (2.2 pounds).

But busy defense lawyers encounter that sort of problem all the time, so judges generally work things out. They did: It was agreed that Light would appear in the Brooklyn courtroom in the mornings, and Manhattan in the afternoons.

Purely routine, except for the fact that the Brooklyn drug defendant was named Martin Light.

(The deal fell apart after several jurors in the Manhattan case read a newspaper account describing the arrangement, forcing declaration of a mistrial.)

Most drug lawyers don't handle the logistics with as much aplomb as did Martin Light, but for many it's a short stumble from criminal defense to criminal defendant. Some even find the war on drugs exploding into a three-front battle:

They simultaneously defend druggies, deal drugs, and do drugs.

But unlike many Bad Lawyer crimes, this one should have been predictable. After all, lawyers are at least as prone to human frailty as the population at large; they can connect with clients who have drugs—and most of whom have easy access to cash. Indeed, given all of that, it would be surprising if lawyers did *not* have widespread problems with drugs.

No surprises here.

Experts say that at least half of all discipline and malpractice cases involving lawyers concern substance abuse. An *ABA Journal* poll shows that 38 percent of lawyers aged twenty-five to thirty-four admit smoking pot at some time in their lives; that seems like a low number, and it turns out that it is, since another 24 percent of the lawyers in that group took the Fifth, refusing to answer the question.

Not surprisingly, then, two thirds of the attorney respondents said pot smoking should not have disqualified Judge Douglas Ginsburg from the United States Supreme Court. The anomaly of lawyers breaking the law, especially with drugs, does not seem to have alarmed the profession, perhaps because it is so commonplace.

A Baltimore lawyer finally kicked his stubborn coke habit by switching to heroin, but managed to represent clients in court under the influence of both drugs. A South Dakota attorney couldn't beat his cocaine habit until he was sentenced to prison for trafficking; he used his clients to help move the drugs.

An Ohio lawyer bought some grass and coke from a client, then credited the client with $150 toward his legal bill. A federal prosecutor in New York drew jail time for stealing cocaine and heroin from the evidence vault. Three New Jersey lawyers clerking for the state superior court were fired for snorting cocaine.

The cases are as diverse as creative lawyers can make them.

But attorney drug-abusers have three advantages in common that distinguish them from their crack-house counterparts:

- Like all addicts, attorneys have to come up with cash for a fix. But unlike ordinary coke-heads, many lawyers have an instant line of credit: client funds.

  New Jersey lawyer Joseph T. Romano drew down on that line, forging another lawyer's signature and snatching at least $11,000 from clients. But that barely got him through the month, since he was hooked on a $2,000-a-week coke habit. He was never charged with a crime (courtesy of the Club?), and argued that his drug addiction should be a mitigating factor against disbarment.

  The New Jersey Supreme Court just said no.

- Having been trained in the law, attorneys don't concede that drug dealing is wrong, even when they get caught.

Florida lawyer Dennis P. Sheppard admitted selling $25,000 worth of marijuana during a month-long period. Did he expect that admission might have implications for his career in the law?

No.

"While acknowledging that his conduct was illegal," the Supreme Court of Florida noted in its opinion ordering disbarment, *"he maintained that it was not morally wrong"*.

That may sound like hairsplitting, but that's the name of the game for a lawyer fighting to save that valuable license to practice. And it certainly distinguished Sheppard from your run-of-the-mill druggie. But as every lawyer would recognize, Sheppard was really sending a secret message to the judges who judged him: Pssst, let's say my crime lacked Moral Turpitude, and let me off, professional courtesy.

The court didn't buy it, and he was disbarred.

Another Sunshine State lawyer had more luck with the Florida Supreme Court (which gets a lot of practice on drug cases). Despite Howard Rosen's double federal felony conviction for cocaine trafficking, the Florida court let him stay in the Club (in contrast to that stern Iowa court that said drug-dealing lawyers did not have the qualities of character required for the bar), with only a three-year suspension.

- Finally, since we make our own rules and police our own profession, we're certainly not about to impose any constitutionally questionable tactics like random drug testing or urine sampling that might reveal the extent of drug abuse in our business.

  Granted, other occupations may require that sort of precaution. We can see why it makes sense for railroad engineers and pilots, and it's certainly understandable for basketball and football players, where the whole integrity of a game is at stake.

  But not for lawyers.

  After all, the only thing at risk here is our system of justice.

In 1989, the United States Supreme Court blew a storm into the sunny world of drug law, ruling in two cases that the government can confiscate money and property gained from criminal activity, even—gasp!—cash earmarked for legal fees.

Prosecutors have long contended that drug clients often pay inflated "legal fees," happily, as a secure way to stash drug cash until it's needed; the defense bar vigorously denies this. In any event, the Court focused squarely on the fee issue, and the majority declared that when Congress passed a strong asset-forfeiture law in 1984 to give force to the old adage that " 'crime does not pay,' " there was no evidence the lawmakers intended to say " 'except for attorney's fees.' "

Criminal defense lawyers would have been happier if the Court had restored public flogging. Indeed, the Supreme Court ruling on fee forfeiture sparked more concern about the impact of drugs in our profession than all of the previous cases of lawyer drug-dealing and attorney addiction—combined.

It's really better to keep it quiet when a lawyer gets a few years in the penalty box, most lawyers believe; that's a private concern for the profession, and we should not undermine public confidence in the administration of justice by broadcasting it about. But when it comes to forfeiting legal fees across the board, depriving innocent clients of the counsel of their choice . . . that is a matter of basic constitutional rights, and every lawyer has an ethical obligation to stand up and be counted.

The National Association of Criminal Defense Lawyers (NACDL) promptly announced a five-point counterattack, along with the creation of two task forces of defense lawyers and constitutional scholars, to "protect and preserve" the adversary criminal justice system.

Stating his objection more candidly, defense lawyer Scott Wallace told *Time* magazine, "No one who has law school loans, a mortgage to pay and kids to feed can afford to practice this kind of law anymore."

True, Scott, but that's not how we make the argument.

NACDL president-elect Neal R. Sonnett put the focus back where it should be, on the Constitution: "I think it is a very dark day for the Sixth Amendment right to counsel and the adversary system of justice," he told the *Philadelphia Inquirer*. "If the Department of Justice views this as a green light to aggressively go after attorney's fees, the result will be that many people accused of crimes will not be able to hire the attorneys of their choice, and it will drive a lot of honest, ethical lawyers out of criminal-defense law."

This is where we came in, with money problems causing a lawyer shortage in criminal defense. For now, though, there's still enough drug money sloshing around the legal profession that most observers see no immediate threat to the Sixth Amendment.

As lawyers, we can all feel good about that.

Oh, by the way, how much cash was involved in the two cases decided by the Supreme Court?

Well, $170,000 in one case, and $400,000 in the other.

Legal fees or drug cash stash?

You be the judge.

Our Secret Rules

(So Secret Even We Don't Know Them)

Armani and Belge discovered—like everyone involved with murder victims—that the bodies are the problem.

Killing is easy.

Guns and knives, uncomplicated and user-friendly, account for more than half of American violent crimes annually. But for killers too squeamish to cut or shoot, there's an almost infinite variety of other ways: strangle, suffocate, poison, push off the roof or in front of the subway, electrocute, run over, car bomb, letter bomb . . . the list goes on.

Organized-crime killers, with professional reps to protect, sometimes go mix-and-match, putting several methods together. Philadelphia mob figure Antonio Rocco Caponigro was tortured, beaten, and shot; then twenty-dollar bills were stuffed into his various body orifices (of which he had several more at the end of the evening than before), to say—if you haven't guessed—GREEDY.

But whatever the technique, once the victim's heart stops, trouble starts.

Rigid or floppy, stiffs are cumbersome. Many killers are not strong enough to carry an adult body, so they have to drag it, leaving an incriminating trail of bowels and blood. Worse, after the excitement of the deed, even murderers who had creative ideas about killing seem to slip back to cliché disposal methods; Caponigro's killers, for example, signed off on their hit the old-fashioned way, leaving his naked body in a car trunk in the Bronx.

The small percentage of killers who are in fact cold-blooded often have elaborate disposal schemes, but what they all have in common is a high rate of failure. Human bodies (or parts) have a way of floating to the river surface, or being sniffed out from their shallow graves by hunting dogs, or discovered in the attic after neighbors report an overpowering stench.

In short, it's extremely difficult to make human bodies *really* disappear, so the overwhelming majority of murder victims get discovered. (Even Jimmy Hoffa, the most notable exception, might rematerialize if they dig up Meadowlands Stadium to build condos one day.)

Frank Armani and Francis Belge thought long and hard about the victims. They knew that everything they had worked for could be undone if they made a slip. With the police already on the case and the father of one victim poking around, asking questions, it would not be easy to keep the bodies secret, but Armani and Belge knew they had no choice.

No one was ever going to link up the bodies with them.

Not surprising, for cold-blooded killers.

Except Armani and Belge were not killers.

They were New York lawyers.

Their client was Robert Garrow, charged in another murder. Preparing an insanity defense with his lawyers, Garrow had confessed to three additional murders, and attorney Belge went out and found the body of Alicia Hauck where Garrow said it would be.

Now what?

It was a complicated question, so Armani and Belge did what lawyers do, they talked to another lawyer. After working through the issues, the three lawyers agreed on what legal ethics required them to do:

Nothing.

They told no one. Even so, rumors seeped out, and the father of one victim, who had flown in from Chicago frantically seeking some clue, showed up at their offices and begged for information. The attorneys told him nothing.

The lawyers' little secret was finally revealed during Garrow's trial, sparking intense public outrage. But it appeared that Belge, at least, would pay the price, since he had obviously violated the New York law that required anyone knowing of the death of a person without medical attendance to report it to authorities, as well as a more obscure statute mandating a decent burial for the dead.

And indeed, the district attorney promptly convened a grand jury, which indicted Belge on those charges.

His indictment was dismissed.

Belge's lips were sealed, the court ruled, by one of our favorite Secret Rules, the one establishing the sanctity of the attorney-client privilege.

While we're generally not so big on celibacy or poverty, lawyers are like priests in one way: We hear lots of guilty secrets, and have rigid requirements about keeping them. So rigid, in fact, that the New York lawyer ethics panel ruled that Belge and Armani would have violated the rules if they *had* disclosed their discovery of the corpse.

Surprising as that may sound, it actually makes perfect sense. If our adversary system is to fully protect individual rights, lawyers must be armed with complete and candid information from their clients. As Belge's trial court ruled: "The effectiveness of counsel is only as great as the confidentiality of its client-attorney relationship. If the lawyer cannot get all of the facts about the case, he can only give his client half of a defense."

In short, any client contemplating a true confession to the counselor is entitled to an ironclad, loophole-free, guarantee that his secret will be secure forever.

It might be possible, of course, to carve out an exception for extreme cases, like murder. But here's the catch: The more despicable the deed, the more important it is to an effective defense that the lawyer know about it. Whether out of embarrassment or mistrust, clients are often tempted to withhold vital facts from their attorney; if there was even a remote possibility that the lawyer might call the cops, they would clam up completely.

Once you think it through, then, it's easy to see why the protection of the attorney-client privilege must be absolute and unconditional. Client confidence is essential, and the Secret Rules spell out the attorney's duty in stern terms.

Simply put, we'll *never* tell.

That means not today, not tomorrow, not even years from now after the client has gone to his eternal reward—no matter how incriminating the circumstances.

For example, even after Boston murder suspect Charles Stuart committed suicide (faced with the unraveling of the elaborate hoax in which he allegedly shot and killed his pregnant wife and their unborn son, then wounded himself), his attorney refused to testify about his final conversation with Stuart—and suggested that he would not break the privilege even if a court ordered him to.

When the attorney-client privilege is on the line, that's the sort of unconditional stand attorneys take. The authorities could rip out our fingernails, hang us by our suspenders until we sing soprano, even audit our tax returns, but we'll never spill your dirty secrets.

Well, hardly ever.

There are a couple of small exceptions that we usually

don't mention when we're giving our sanctity-of-the-attorney-client-privilege speech.

"A lawyer may reveal such information," Rule 1.6 states, ". . . to establish a claim or defense on behalf of the lawyer in a controversy between the lawyer and the client, to establish a defense to a criminal charge or civil claim or disciplinary proceeding against the lawyer based upon conduct in which the client was involved, or to respond to allegations in any proceeding concerning the lawyer's representation of the client."

What does *that* mean?

The prior version of the Secret Rules sheds some light, since the comparable provision was considerably more forthright (that is probably why it required revision):

"A lawyer *may* reveal confidences or secrets," the old rule provided, "necessary to establish or collect his fee or to defend himself or his employees or associates against an accusation of wrongful conduct."

Aha.

Back to basics.

Hushing up murder is one thing; that's our professional responsibility to the client. But legal fees and malpractice suits . . . whoaaaa, now you're talking money. That's an entirely different matter. We'll protect confidences within reason, but clients who want to mistreat their lawyer cannot expect to hide behind the attorney-client privilege.

Bottom line, we'll cover your crimes every time, but whiners and deadbeats beware: Your secrets aren't sacred if you bad-mouth your barrister, or stiff him on a fee.

The Secret Rules are almost straightforward if you keep one fact sharply in focus: They did not come from Mount Sinai—instead, we write them.

Lawyers decide what lawyers are allowed to do. At first blush, that may seem a little like letting Jesse James design the bank security system, but it's really not so unusual. Doctors define medical ethics, after all; engineers set their professional standards; even funeral directors and beauticians abide by voluntary, industry-generated codes of conduct.

But there are two big distinctions. First, when the building collapses or the patient convulses into an allergic reaction, the engineer or doctor will eventually have to justify both his actions and his profession's standards of conduct to hard-eyed, contingent-fee-chasing lawyers, and ultimately, to a lawyer-trained judge.

But happily, it does not work the other way. We never have to answer to the doctors (whew!), and even when lawyers sue fellow lawyers, those hard eyes soften a little; it's all in the Club.

The other difference is that while funeral directors and beauticians may make some of their own rules, they are also typically licensed and regulated by a state agency, composed of people who are *not* in the burial or beauty business.

With this background, ask yourself a question: If free from outside meddlers, you could write the rules that would largely determine how much money you could make from your occupation, what would your rules look like?

Probably a lot like ours.

Indeed, you might even begin the way we did, with no rules at all. American lawyers did not adopt a common code of conduct until 1908, much later than most professions, a full half-century after doctors swallowed hard and took their medicine. But having adopted the original ABA Canons of Ethics, lawyers did what lawyers do: argued, revised, disputed, redrafted, dissected, proposed, objected.

The 1969 ABA Code of Professional Responsibility eventually resulted, after which we started over, coming up, in 1983, with the Model Rules of Professional Conduct. (And stay tuned, we're back at it again.)

Why so many revisions?

Let's look at the evolution of Rule 1.6, that old favorite that protects the confidentiality of information. Stripped of legalese, the central issue was simple. Should lawyers, like all other citizens who see a crime shaping up, dial 911?

The old rule *allowed* (but did not require) lawyers to disclose a client's plan to commit a crime—any crime. For folks in the law business, that seems like a fairly relaxed standard, and some ABA members thought it should be tougher. After all, if Jack the Ripper tells his lawyer he's going to slash up victim number 12 tonight, is the attorney's only option to check the obituaries in the morning?

That concern led to a big push in the ABA for a rule that would have *required* an attorney to blow the whistle on Jack the Ripper. But trial lawyers, whose clients are often in the crime business, screamed like mugging victims, and a six-year tug-of-war followed.

Here's how it went:

Old Rule	Allowed Disclosure	Of Client's Intention to Commit Crime
Early Draft	Required Disclosure	To Prevent Death or Serious Bodily Harm
Later Draft	Allowed Disclosure	To Prevent Death, Substantial Bodily Harm, or Financial Injury
New Rule Adopted by ABA	Allows Disclosure	To Prevent Imminent Death or Substantial Bodily Harm

The trial lawyers won.

A lawyer is *allowed* to turn in Jack the Ripper only if the crime is going to be "imminent" and fatal—or at least very bloody. Even then, if he decides to keep quiet, the Secret Rules say that's okay too.

And if the criminal is Ivan Boesky instead of Jack the

Ripper, and the crime is a $100-million stock fraud, the new Rules say the lawyer is not allowed to tell anyone.

As in all Secret Rules, it's important to pay close attention to the Weasel Words, which generally add the backspin that makes the rule mean the opposite of what you would have thought. To permit disclosure under the "imminent death" exception, then, we're talking murder *now,* today—not next week, maybe not even tomorrow. "Substantial bodily harm" has to hurt a lot more than "serious bodily harm." "Shall" means something should happen; "may" means it could, but won't.

And the reason lawyers are constantly tinkering with the Secret Rules is that even a single one of those little Weasel Words has the potential to make or break practitioners in a given area of the law.

So we've gone from no rules to a kaleidoscopic maze of rules—Canons, then Code, now Model Rules, further blurred by a constant flux of state-by-state exceptions. Some lawyers, inevitably, get caught in the switches.

New Jersey practitioner Donald H. Mintz, for example, suspended under the Code, might have had a free pass under the Model Rules. Attorney Mintz, tired of being threatened by his lover's six-foot-three, three-hundred-pound former husband (who also happened to be a previous Mintz divorce client), had an idea. One of his other clients, Mintz thought, had connections.

Mintz was right.

Client Anthony Cappolla had a long rap sheet, and knew some wise guys. Unfortunately for Mintz, however, Cappolla's rap sheet was long enough to convince him to wear a wire for the prosecutor. When he next met with his lawyer (who tried to pat him down like they do on TV but missed the mike), they discussed bringing in a female contract killer from Canada to solve Mintz's problem.

Attorney Mintz was enthusiastic. "Can you imagine what dynamite," the mouthpiece said into the hidden mike, "what dynamite a female, a beautiful female killer would be?"

The scheme with Cappolla did not pose any obvious ethical problem for Mintz, since no one had thought to write a rule saying lawyers should not ask clients to hire Canadian hit women to kill other clients. Still, it seemed like there must be *something* wrong with Mintz's flirtation with a hired gun, and New Jersey officials finally decided it adversely reflected on his fitness to practice law, in violation of Rule 1–102 (A) (6). (He got off with a gentle two-year suspension, on the theory he was only "fantasizing.")

Mintz should have waited.

The Model Rules eliminated the adversely-reflects-on-fitness-to-practice provision, which critics called "a vague and loose standard." (The critics were right, of course, which is why it was a good rule; since the imagination of rule breakers consistently outruns that of rule makers, some Bad Lawyers will only get caught by a catchall provision.)

Even if the omission of the fitness-to-practice rule looks like a step backward, most lawyers believe that our relentless quest for the perfect set of rules *is* improving the legal profession. Critics, though, contend that many rules for lawyers are not designed to make lawyers behave better at all; they're intended to curtail competition and protect the lawyer monopoly.

For years, we shrugged this off, confident that as a "learned profession," we had antitrust immunity. (The inherent contradiction of conducting legal practice *like a business* to jack up profits, even while claiming professional status to avoid antitrust laws, seems to have passed unnoticed.)

In 1975, however, a unanimous United States Supreme Court rocked the learned profession by ruling that the Virginia Bar Association's minimum fee schedule violated federal antitrust laws.

Antitrust law is a highly complex field. Most lawyers know next to nothing about it. But *all* lawyers can give you two words' worth of wisdom about antitrust: *treble damages*. Antitrust winners get three times more money than ordinary lawsuit winners.

Fine.

Plaintiff's lawyers love it. Other lawyers, being in the Club, accept it. Economists think the stiff penalties make markets work. But no one in the legal profession wants to be—*personally,* we're not talking about client money here—on the paying end of an antitrust situation.

Since 1975, then, lawyers have been scrambling to stay ahead of the feds. Minimum fees were jettisoned instantly, and, reeling from a second adverse Supreme Court ruling, the profession decided that advertising by lawyers was not unethical, after all.

Then in 1978, spooked by a Justice Department antitrust action that claimed the Secret Rules were limiting competition among lawyers, the ABA told the G-men, in effect, "Hey guys, just kidding about these rules, heh, heh."

To prove it, as part of a negotiated settlement of the federal charges, the ABA Code of Professional Responsibility was renamed, becoming the *Model* Code of Professional Responsibility (and the later Rules of Professional Conduct became the *Model* Rules of Professional Conduct).

The idea was that the ABA rules, in their various versions, were only *examples* of rules someone might want to adopt, maybe useful for states like Montana that didn't have enough lawyers for a big committee to write their own rules, certainly *not* the Secret Rules of a closed Club. (That theory wore a little thin, however, when, one after the other, states started adopting the Model Rules with only minor variations—as they had all previously enacted the Model

Code. But maybe they all simply thought it was a good example.)

For now, the antitrust heat seems to be off, but it will certainly be turned back up at some point. When that happens, though, the feds may be surprised to learn that we've been holding a trump card in reserve. In fact, we have a perfect defense:

How can our Secret Rules have any anticompetitive impact when—except for the relative handful of ABA activists who keep revising them—not one lawyer in ten has any concrete idea what's in them?

While keeping the feds at bay, we've also had to fend off attacks on lawyer rules from within the profession. And not only from maniacs like Ralph Nader. Establishment lawyer Peter Megargee Brown, for example, told an ABA commission in 1985: "Ninety percent of lawyers who do not go into court with any regularity are, seated at their office desks, virtually undisciplined by any meaningful code of responsibility."

But just a glance at the Table of Contents of the Model Rules indicates that that charge hardly seems fair. In addition to more than a dozen detailed provisions about the client-lawyer relationship generally (covering topics such as lawyer competence, conflicts of interest, fees, safekeeping property, and confidentiality), there are separate sets of rules defining the duties of lawyers as counselor, advocate, in law firms and associations, and in public service. There's even a section called "Maintaining the Integrity of the Profession," and while it's only four pages (out of seventy-nine), its inclusion is proof of our commitment.

Our Secret Rules, in short, cover the legal landscape.

Still, lawyers who wear three-piece names and give speeches to the ABA titled "The Quiet Revolution in the American Law Profession" do not generally make wild and crazy charges, so what was Peter Megargee Brown trying to say?

"Meaningful"—that must be the key.

Maybe his point was that lawyers are "virtually undisciplined by any *meaningful* code of responsibility."

But given the heated ABA debates, the endless redrafts and revisions, indeed, the sheer *number* of ethical rules lawyers have to live by, that would seem pretty unlikely.

Except for this one key fact:

Lawyers, remember, write the rules for lawyers.

We also read them.

If you complain to your state disciplinary board about your attorney's conduct, and make it past the summary blow-out process, it will be a lawyer who reads the Secret Rules to see if your charges are actionable.

There's nothing surprising in that. But once the disciplinary board lawyer is finished reading the Secret Rules that apply to your case, what he decides might come as a surprise, because one of the big advantages of law school is that we learn some reading tricks that no one else knows.

Let's take a quick look at how lawyers read rules.

We've already seen how the ethical ban on excessive fees did not slow down a New York firm from billing a reported $20 million for two weeks' work.

Why?

Because the rule only prohibits *clearly* excessive fees.

If you want to read like we do, stop skipping over words; every single word is important.

With that in mind, let's practice rule reading with Rule 3.2, which is called "Expediting Litigation."

"A lawyer shall make *reasonable* efforts to expedite litigation *consistent with the interests of the client*."

That should speed up those lawsuits, right?

Wrong again.

"Reasonable" is an obvious Weasel Word, but the real escape hatch is the last clause. Litigation produces two results: one winner and one loser. Most times, the lawyers have a pretty accurate idea of who will be which a long time before trial.

Pretend you are a client: Is it consistent with your interests to lose today, if that's what is likely to happen, or would you prefer, say, about five years from today? When two clients fight in court, at least one of them usually has an interest in making things go slowly.

Let's try another one.

"Rule 3.3 Candor Toward Tribunal: A lawyer shall not *knowingly* offer evidence that the lawyer *knows* to be *false*."

"Knowingly . . . knows" gives it away.

A lawyer can tell a tale to the tribunal that smells like bad bluefish, as long as he doesn't *know* it's phony. To play this game, barristers become more agile than ballerinas in pirouetting around questions that might lead to knowing inconvenient facts.

Not being trained in the law, clients sometimes miss the subtle nuances of this exercise. An Iowa murderer, for example, bluntly asked his lawyer to assist in giving false trial testimony. That was a wrong step in the dance, and the attorney, correctly, refused. The killer then claimed his constitutional right to assistance of counsel had been violated, and appealed his conviction to the United States Supreme Court.

The high court turned down the appeal, ruling unanimously that an attorney is not obligated to assist clients in committing perjury. Five of the justices went even further, stating that the lawyer should either convince his client not to lie, or disclose his intentions to the judge. That provoked a heated objection from the other four justices.

Odd, when you think about it, that the specter of lawyers urging clients to tell the truth would get four justices of the United States Supreme Court so excited: "Unfortunately," Justice William J. Brennan, Jr., wrote, "the court seems unable to resist the temptation of sharing with the legal community its vision of ethical conduct." Now, nonlawyers may not immediately understand why sharing a vision of ethical conduct is a temptation to be resisted, especially when the people doing it are Supreme Court justices. But Brennan was emphatic: "The court's essay regarding what constitutes the correct response to a criminal client's suggestion that he will perjure himself," the justice added, "is pure discourse without force of law."

But then, as I learned from the Pennsylvania lawyer disciplinary board while I was federal prosecutor, telling the truth is not necessarily a good idea under the Secret Rules.

A firebomb exploded into the home of Radames Santiago in a racially tense Philadelphia neighborhood. By the time the predawn blaze was extinguished, five persons inside were dead.

The district attorney launched an all-out investigation, with the prime suspect being a slightly retarded neighbor, Robert "Reds" Wilkinson. After an intensive interrogation, the police got a confession.

Then it all blew apart.

A judge threw out Wilkinson's confession, ruling that the mildly retarded defendant had not understood his constitutional rights. Still, Wilkinson was convicted of the five murders and sent to jail, based on the testimony of a fourteen-year-old eyewitness, Nelson Garcia. But then Garcia recanted, and told a federal grand jury he had lied about Wilkinson's involvement. At that point, Wilkinson was released, which meant that someone had killed five people and gotten away with it.

Our office initiated a federal civil rights probe, bossed by one of the most able prosecutors I've ever known, Criminal Division chief Gil Scutti. When Scutti was finished, a man named David McGinnis (whose prior confession to Philadelphia prosecutors had been literally thrown away because it did not implicate Wilkinson) had been sentenced to twenty-two years in federal prison after admitting that he threw the firebomb. Ronald Hanley, a local political figure, was convicted of plotting the crime and jailed.

Throughout the intensive federal investigation, not one shred of evidence implicating Wilkinson was discovered. The *Philadelphia Inquirer*, in a Pulitzer Prize–winning investigative series, established that at least seven persons had been beaten or otherwise coerced into making false statements.

After McGinnis testified in federal court that "I decided I wanted to get it off my back and to get Reds Wilkinson out of jail 'cause he had nothing to do with it" but that the district attorney's office had discarded the tape recording of his confession, the chief judge of the United States district court exploded, on the record: "I think it is an outrage what the District Attorney of Philadelphia did here, an absolute outrage. . . . This jury has a right to know that under the Constitution of the United States the District Attorney violated his oath of office and violated the Constitution."

A short time later, the district attorney reindicted Wilkinson.

Asked my reaction, I said that the DA's action was "outrageous" and "unbelievable." A state court judge apparently agreed, quickly dismissing the indictment on grounds of "prosecutorial misconduct."

The Santiago case and trials of Reds Wilkinson, both later featured on a network television show, were finally over.

Actually, not quite.

Six months later, I received a "Personal and Confidential" certified letter from the Disciplinary Board of the Supreme Court of Pennsylvania. In six single-spaced pages of charges, it stated that the district attorney had accused me of professional misconduct, and advised that "you may wish to consult with counsel before replying to this letter."

Consult with counsel?

I thought we were the good guys.

Our office had freed an innocent man, convicted two other defendants in the arson-murders of five people, and laid bare police abuse and prosecutorial misconduct in the process. At the end of that, I might require counsel to hang on to my license to practice?

Yes.

Why?

Because, as I discovered after reviewing the Secret Rules cited in the letter, calling an outrageous indictment "outrageous" is not the sort of observation that is encouraged by the legal profession. Doctors bury their mistakes, and while we don't usually have that option, we do have a whole series of rules designed to keep lawyers quiet about lawyers' blunders.

One catchall, prominently cited in the Disciplinary Board letter, is "conduct prejudicial to the administration of justice." Nonlawyers should pay close attention here, because beginners often have trouble with this notion. How could criticism of the *re*indictment of a man judicially determined to be innocent somehow be prejudicial to the administration of *justice*?

But lawyers will understand right away.

The point is that, right or wrong, we don't want a lot of second-guessing about our lawyering. We may not be able to muzzle the general public, but we certainly can limit critical comment by members of the Club, and that's exactly what the Secret Rules do. The Disciplinary Board also charged me with making an "extrajudicial statement" in a criminal matter; again, in English, that means I had broken the speak-no-evil code of the Club.

After a few lawyerly volleys of paperwork with the

Disciplinary Board, I received a private reprimand. At least that's my best recollection. I can no longer locate the actual piece of paper, and—as is the experience of many lawyers who have a brush with professional discipline—it did not leave much of a lasting impression.

"Take Off Your Clothes" and Other Unusual Legal Advice

Sweet P.

That's what Frick called Peggy, when he wrote. Except when he addressed her as "My dear, sweet P." Or "cocksucker."

Actually, he didn't *call* her "cocksucker." That word was spray-painted onto her house, shortly after Peggy received an anonymous letter (later determined to be from Frick) predicting vandalism, even correctly guessing the paint color. Also, on the night her house was sprayed, a rock was thrown through Peggy's bedroom window and her porch light was painted red.

"Whore" was scratched into the paint on her car, the same word spray-painted several times on her jeep, and the brothers at a local fraternity received an anonymous letter suggesting they call P to have "a good time."

But Frick was not afraid to sign his name to a letter. He signed one calling P a "one-hour punching bag," and a "midnite barroom pickup."

"Your looks will begin to go," he wrote Peggy on another occasion, "those gorgeous breasts will begin to sag, the double chin and tenderloin will become permanent. . . ."

And there were many more defamatory letters, plenty to work with, if P wanted to engage a lawyer.

She did.

In fact, she already had.

He was a widely esteemed Missouri practitioner, almost thirty years Peggy's senior. He had handled her divorce, and later, when he encountered some personal difficulty of his own, 142 prominent citizens and 68 lawyers were willing to stand up for him.

That difficulty was a disbarment proceeding based on the lawyer's harassment of a former client. The client's name, masked in court records to protect her identity, was Peggy ———.

The lawyer's name was William Y. Frick.

In the end, attorney Frick's behavior was a little extreme.

When the security guards finally caught him, Frick was busy with his hobby, spray-painting Peggy's name on the Northeast Missouri State University campus.

"Stand back and give me room," the distinguished lawyer snarled, trying a Clint Eastwood line, and when that didn't work he pulled out a pistol and squeezed off a couple of shots. Both missed, but the attempt earned him a felony conviction, which—along with the vandalism and harassment of his former client—resulted in his disbarment.

But in the beginning, he was simply a lawyer in love. And despite the frequent caricature of lawyers as cold, unfeeling, hard-hearted hired guns, the fact is that many lawyers have romantic feelings too. Indeed, because we normally keep our emotions under such rigid control, it's not widely understood that lawyers, like everyone else, can be zapped—by a moonlit night, a secret glance, that special kiss.

Wisconsin attorney Thomas Edward Martin felt the magic.

For Martin, it wasn't Paris in the springtime, but Chicago, and then Milwaukee, in the fall. With carefree abandon, the lawyer and his lover caroused their way through both cities, drinking, partying, making love.

It was all foolish and crazy.

But unlike attorney Frick, Martin was at least careful not to get involved with a client.

Martin's lover was a fourteen-year-old boy.

But wait, he could explain.

The kid lied about his age; he looked older. (Like, maybe sixteen, Counselor?)

Martin also argued that he did not contribute to the boy's absence from home because the kid was already away from home when he picked him up, and that his acts, "while unlawful, are not morally reprehensible." (Sound familiar? Just another version of our old standby, Moral Turpitude.)

The Wisconsin Supreme Court, noting that Martin "enjoys an excellent reputation for competence and character in the legal community in Milwaukee," nevertheless concluded that his extracurricular activities constituted "unprofessional conduct." His license to practice was suspended for six months.

Lawyers and sex.

Who cares?

After all, William Frick was not the first over-the-hill male to go ga-ga over a young girl, and attorney Martin's crime would have been the same if he had been an architect or a truck driver. On the surface, the sexual peccadillos of lawyers would not seem to deserve special attention. Anyone who reads bumper stickers knows that every occupation in America takes pride in its amatory prowess

(Carpenters Have the Best Tools; Divers Do It Deeper; Everyone, it would seem, Does It with Wishful Thinking), so we could just say Lawyers Do It in Their Briefs, and move on.

But three features of lawyer sex make it worth pausing to take a peek at how it happens, and what the profession does in response.

- In contrast to firemen and accountants and almost everyone else (except doctors), lawyers often find an opportunity for dalliances in the line of duty. That's because, as we've seen, desperate clients will do whatever the barrister demands, and with unscrupulous lawyers, the usual options are big cash fees, drugs, or sex.

  Forced sex, in short, can happen *solely because the lawyer is a lawyer.* When an attorney makes a move behind closed doors, then, it's rarely a private affair between consenting adults (even when both parties *are* adults). More likely, it's a lawyer abusing his position of trust, and the abuses run from rape to sexual harassment, and everything in between.

- The second surprise: Lawyer-client sex is okay.

  We don't advertise that, of course.

  But it's not too hard to figure out if you read our Secret Rules, since they not only don't impose any limits on lawyers having sexual relationships with clients, they don't even mention the subject.

  And while we sometimes stray from holy writ in other areas, when colleagues in the Club reveal weakness of the flesh, our general reaction is that any stones cast should come from lawyers without sin.

  That means we usually go easy.

  That's why Indiana attorney Jack Wood, who, as we've seen, bartered legal services for sex and dirty pictures, was not disbarred, but only suspended. He was soon back in practice, up to his old tricks. The next time, his victim was not a client, but the seventeen-year-old niece of a friend of his client. Attorney Wood agreed that the teenager's commercial potential could cover his legal fees, and he was willing to introduce her to some friends in business.

Their business was called Naked City.

Set up by a lawyer, the seventeen-year-old starred in pornographic movies until the violence got too scary.

Attorney Wood finally got disbarred.

- Finally, even when caught in flagrante delicto with our pants (or skirts) down, lawyers often dance past punishment, because, being lawyers, we can always explain.

  If you were caught delivering $2,500 in cash payoffs to a police inspector to keep your paramour's massage parlor open, for example, there's a high likelihood that you would be reading this in a prison library somewhere. But, as we'll see, when Philadelphia lawyer Joseph H. Weiss found himself in that predicament, he picked up on something in the situation that nonlawyers probably would have missed.

  Weiss recognized that he was the *victim*.

Contrary to the conventional assumption, philandering attorneys are *not* concentrated mostly in a particular practice area. But if they were, and you had to guess which one, the odds are about 100 to 1 you would pick divorce lawyers—who have lately tried to upgrade their image by calling what they do family law (un-family law would be closer to it). It's easy to see why they're the usual suspects. Exactly 50 percent of divorce clients are female, most are highly vulnerable emotionally, and all are about to be single again.

(Many divorce lawyers are also female, of course, and the vast majority of divorcees are not interested in hopping into bed with any lawyer, male or female. But when it does happen, in cases reported to date, *male* lawyers are overwhelmingly the initiators of sexual contact with their clients, so the assumption here is that that's the normal pattern.)

Divorce lawyers also have an easy opening. What their clients want to discuss differs from client talk with attorneys in other specialties. Kristi does not come to the office to discuss the tax implications of her generation-skipping trust, or to review the termination provision in paragraph 3.47 of the collective bargaining agreement, or to rework the "Management Discussion and Analysis" section of SEC Form 10-K.

Kristi wants to talk about Bob.

But not right away.

What she says in the beginning, in a brave voice with her mascara still perfect, is that everyone knows something like 50 percent of the marriages in this country don't work, at least not forever, and we're going to be civilized adults about this. Two of our closest friends had great marriages, but then horrible divorces, it was like they *hated* each other, we're not going to do that, we plan to stay friends. . . .

The lawyer waits, sympathetic, making notes, or maybe not. (Most of us grab a yellow legal pad as soon as anyone starts talking, but that's generally a prop to convince you we're real lawyers, since it's not often that we go back and read our notes.) But either way, it does not matter, because the lawyer knows what's coming next.

Bob.

I *hate* THAT SOB!

No, no I didn't mean that, I love him, or I loved . . . but I *knew* he was cheating, he thought I was so dumb I couldn't figure it out, but I knew that little bimbo . . . oh, I'm sorry, give me a second to get myself together . . . he can do whatever he wants, fine, we're adults, but how am I supposed to keep these kids in school with no money, I gave him every penny I saved before we got married, probably the bimbo got it all . . . oh, I'm sorry, I didn't mean to do this, I'm going to be okay, I'm going to . . .

Oooohhh.

I'm really sorry, but it just *hurts* so much. . . .

There, there.

Well, what are we *supposed* to do?

Law school doesn't give any guidance (especially schools like Harvard, which rate lawyers doing divorce, or even family law, somewhere south of those doing slip-and-fall). So we have to learn by doing, and after all those snide cocktail party slurs about lawyers being cold-blooded mercenaries, it's only human to want to be . . . uh, a little warmer.

"Brenda" was devastated.

Her husband had simply vanished, she told New York lawyer Darrell Bowen, and their two young children were gone too, along with the family car and credit cards. Then she discovered that every dollar of their savings had been withdrawn too, all without any warning.

Bowen would file the divorce complaint right away, of course, but that seemed like small comfort; it would take time to work its way through the courts, and Brenda needed help right *now*.

Bowen stroked her hair consolingly, and said how nice she looked.

Sex came next.

Another Bowen client was dumped at the bus station by her husband, who tossed ten dollars at her and told her to take a bus back to her parents in Arkansas.

New York to Arkansas for ten dollars?!

Bowen comforted her by having her spend the night at his house.

Bowen told the disciplinary panel that his "judgmental indiscretions" were caused by overdoses of medication for manic depression, which was a nice reversal of the old love-made-me-crazy line. He got a two-year suspension.

Prince of Palimony Marvin Mitchelson did more than pal around with two of his clients, according to charges they made on the CBS program *60 Minutes*. Kristen Barrett-Whitney said that Mitchelson accepted her $25,000 retainer and then raped her in the bathroom; former client

Patricia French also claimed that the lawyer raped her. Mitchelson hotly denied everything, calling the women "professional extortionists." A California victims' compensation board believed them enough to award a reported $56,000 for medical and psychiatric care.

While divorce lawyers have the most obvious opportunities and get most of the blame, other attorneys also find plenty of chances to play the game. It's all because of lusty lawyer libidos, you might (and we like to) imagine, but in fact, there's a much more basic explanation: Lawyers, in nearly every practice area, often deal with people who are simply not in a position to say no.

Even a world away from the supercharged emotions of battling ex-spouses, in the staid halls of academe, attorneys can take advantage. At the William Mitchell College of Law in Minnesota, the dean used his deanship as a social icebreaker, according to four women who charged that he made "unwelcome physical contact and verbal communication of a sexual nature."

But although they all unwillingly endured the dean's touching, squeezing, rubbing, the women—two of them law students—were reluctant witnesses.

"I felt that there would be strong repercussions that could potentially harm, disgrace, or end my career," one of them explained. "I was just a first-year student . . . and Dean Peters had all the power."

"Professional suicide," another student feared. "Dean Peters was a powerful man with a lot of influential friends. I couldn't take the risk."

The dean's own lawyer characterized him as the "tactile dean" (a curious defense strategy, since that's what the case was all about), and Dean Geoffrey Peters received a public reprimand.

Big Firms do it by the numbers.

At least that's what happened in one firm, where male

partners, according to an *ABA Journal* account, kept score by carving notches on their desks when they slept with female lawyers and paralegals.

In all Big Firms, the partners have enormous power over associates. During the decade-long grind to partnership, when six-day workweeks are standard and twenty-hour workdays not uncommon, partners dictate everything from work schedules to memo formats to dress codes—and any associate misstep, or even reluctance, can spell career disaster.

Do partners abuse this power by making sexual advances?

The *National Law Journal,* polling female attorneys in Big Firms in thirteen major cities, asked how many had experienced unwanted sexual attention. Sixty percent of the female lawyers, nearly two out of three, claimed that they had, a response that casts serious doubt on the validity of the poll.

After all, these ladies are in the law business. If they were *really* offended, as one woman lawyer wrote to the Florida Gender Bias Task Force, by male lawyers "looking up my dress if I am going upstairs or down my blouse if I happen to lean over in his presence," they have the perfect weapon. Instead of writing to the task force, any aggrieved woman should describe her problem in a sex discrimination complaint, slap a blue backer on it, and file it in federal court.

But first, she should pay off her law school loans.

Because by the time the case is tried four or five years from now, the partners will have exercised their power to make certain she is a *former* Big Firm lawyer, and the average pay for that is about $35,000 a year to start (instead of the $80,000-plus paid by Big Firms).

And she should also be aware that these cases can take some unpredictable bounces.

The outcome will depend on the specific facts, of course,

but there could be some surprises. That's because it's going to boil down to her word against that of a respected partner, who is almost certain to argue that whatever happened was consensual.

That's all going to get a little personal, but it will not be nearly as embarrassing as the other tactic he'll use for defense, which will be to introduce evidence about the plaintiff's *other* sexual activity. After all, if Jack Litman could do it with a dead murder victim, the Big Firm's defense counsel will not have any compunction against trying it on a live plaintiff.

On balance then, maybe the sex discrimination suit is not such a great idea for Big-Firm female lawyers. The better course might be to report the partner's sexual harassment to the local lawyer disciplinary authorities.

Except that, since our Secret Rules are silent on sex, it's not clear that sexual harassment is a prohibited lawyer activity.

Doctors did it.

Psychologists did too.

Both professions adopted rules of ethics banning sex with patients, the key feature of each rule being that a patient's consent to sex is no defense to a violation of the rule. The obvious notion is that the doctor-patient relationship is so inherently one-sided that consent is never really voluntary. And in the rare cases of true love, where the chemistry is perfect and sparks fly like Fourth of July fireworks, it's not that hard to find another doctor.

Could the legal profession adopt a rule like that?

Technically, yes. In fact, at least one state has considered such a proposal, which would ban even consensual sexual activity between attorneys and clients in cases such as divorce, child-custody, and probate, where clients are generally highly vulnerable.

But don't look for that to mushroom into a national movement. Unlike doctors and shrinks, being in the business of laws and rules, we understand that adopting some draconian ban on basic human impulses will create more problems than it solves; it simply won't work.

For starters, how would you enforce it?

The typical proposal calls for suspending or disbarring the offending attorney. That should thoroughly confuse everyone. We have lawyers who have committed crimes ranging from fraud to drug trafficking, embezzlement to bribery and worse, yet they're still in good standing; now we're going to kick attorneys out of the Club for being *in love*?!

Come, now.

But isn't it usually more lust than love?

Probably—but so what?

Let's try some clear thinking here. Vulnerability is a nice fuzzy concept, but the fact is, vulnerable or not, adults can consent to have sex with each other, even if one of them happens to be an attorney. If the lawyer's position is so awe-inspiring (which we doubt) that the consent is, in reality, involuntary, then it's rape, and we already have a law against that.

But rather than prejudging it, let's see how a rule against attorney-client sex would actually work in practice.

It would not have helped David Jackson. He was unaware, at the time he was convicted of a couple of major felonies, that his defense lawyer and the prosecutor were also a couple. They dated during his trial, going to dinner and the movies, as they had for more than eight months before. The record does not say whether they had sex, but even if they did, it would have been attorney-attorney sex, outside the rule.

(Jackson won a new trial, even though it's not clear how he was prejudiced. After all, what most criminal clients look for in a lawyer is not rarefied jurisprudential wisdom but rather some backdoor hook into the judge or prosecutor; on that score, Jackson hit the jackpot.)

Another attorney was disbarred because of a pattern of sex abuse, but his behavior would not have violated the proposed rule. That's because his victims were not clients, but clients' children, usually about ten or twelve years old.

Nor would a nix on client sex have been much comfort to Richard Erickson. According to the Supreme Court of Minnesota, his estranged wife repeatedly had sexual intercourse with Clement H. Snyder, Jr., who happened to be the Minnesota judge assigned to rule on their marriage breakup. At one point, when he wanted to whisk Mrs. Erickson away to a judges' meeting in Minneapolis, Judge Snyder phonied up a document suggesting she was at a legal secretarial course at William Mitchell College of Law (also home of the "tactile dean"—maybe they should test the water there).

Judge Snyder drew a censure, but his sex was judge-and-litigant, no rule against that.

What about sex with a judge and Mrs. X?

That was how Alabama disciplinary authorities delicately characterized Judge Johnny Langley's partner, but ol' Judge Johnny himself was somewhat less inhibited. He just jumped up and did it with Mrs. X, right there on top of the bench in his courtroom, and then he took some pictures of her dressed, sort of, "in a partially open flannel shirt."

The resulting furor was enough to convince Langley to resign from the bench and surrender his license to practice.

But the judge's little sexcapade would not have violated a rule against attorney-client sex, even if we had one, which we don't and probably won't anytime soon.

"Improper, stupid, unethical, illegal, indiscreet and unprofessional" was how Joe Weiss described his own conduct. That would have been a healthy dose of self-criticism even for an errant intellectual in Chairman Mao's China, but for a highly confident Philadelphia lawyer, it was remarkable.

It was also smart for Weiss to say he was stupid, because that whole litany spelled REMORSE, and if a lawyer is trying to hang on to his license to practice after a brush with the law, remorse is an excellent thing to be overcome by.

Not all attorneys understand this. In Colorado, after he was convicted of sexual assault on a child "less than fifteen years of age" (which meant the victim was between one and fourteen), attorney Dennis Reed Grenemyer told the disciplinary panel that he had not "knowingly" committed a crime, because his sex partner had lied about his age. (Sound familiar?) The lawyer also bristled about how his "personal trust" had been betrayed by his young friend, and argued that he, Grenemyer, was the actual victim.

Remorseless attorney Grenemyer was disbarred.

Remorseful attorney Weiss—who also claimed to be a victim—was not.

Wait a second.

Why would a *victim* be *remorseful*?

Victims are usually devastated or angry or incoherent, and people who are remorseful have generally done something wrong.

How could attorney Weiss be both at once?

That was the tricky part, but being an innovative lawyer, Weiss had a creative approach to the problem. It was not creative enough' it turned out, to persuade the Pennsylvania Office of Disciplinary Counsel (which recommends discipline for lawyer misconduct), but good enough for the state disciplinary board and the Supreme Court of Pennsylvania, which have the final word.

Here's what happened.

Attorney Weiss had a client we'll call Cheryl B., who

wanted to open a massage parlor, the kind—they both knew—that would *not* limit its services to those aching back and shoulder muscles. Weiss set up the corporation, called Ozzie-Oz, Inc., and arranged for a $25,000 start-up loan, at a whopping 24 percent interest.

Next, concerned that the Philadelphia police might bust the joint, Weiss asked another client to set up a meeting for him with the police inspector. According to the subsequent court opinion, Weiss delicately asked the inspector whether his client "should be concerned about police activity" (not having been there, we don't know what got said, but you can bet it was not that), and the top cop replied, in effect, $500 a month, no problem.

A short time later, Weiss delivered five $100 bills, given to him by Cheryl B., to the police inspector. At that meeting, the inspector also introduced Weiss to his lieutenant.

The next month, attorney Weiss delivered ten more C-notes from Cheryl B. to the lieutenant.

Two months later, Weiss delivered another $1,000 from Ozzie-Oz to the police inspector.

Six months after that, Weiss was questioned by FBI agents as part of a federal probe into police corruption. He denied any involvement with the police inspector, and denied any knowledge of involvement with anyone associated with Ozzie-Oz.

The feds told Weiss they had evidence that he was not being completely truthful.

Trapped, Weiss confessed. He also agreed to testify as a prosecution witness against the police, which bought him a free pass on possible criminal charges.

But even after he had testified as a cooperating government witness, Weiss faced a major problem. The lawyer disciplinary board was sure to hear about his testimony; how could he explain paying off police to protect prostitution, without being kicked out of the legal profession?

It was not an immediate problem, though, because it

would take the disciplinary board more than five years to follow up with Weiss. And that meant he had time to come up with an answer.

When he finally testified before the disciplinary panel, Weiss opened dramatically: "I don't know whether any of you have ever been in love in your lives. I assume that you have, and I assume that you understand, therefore, the crazy things that somebody may do . . . when they are in love."

Cutting through the drama, Joe said it was all because he was nuts about Cheryl.

He had not mentioned that to the FBI or anyone else previously, but it was, after all, kind of personal. Now, he was coming clean, admitting that he was head-over-heels crazy for his client Cheryl B., not just in love but consumed, victim of a tempestuous, white-hot passion, obsessed by the intensity of their sizzling romance, powerless to resist her desires.

He also explained that he had been *extorted* by the cops, which meant he was the *victim,* which was why he had initially lied about making the payoffs, because "of fear for his personal safety from the high-ranking police officers with whom he had dealt."

Weiss went on to say that he had found himself caught "between two extremely powerful forces—my lover on the one hand and a very powerful police inspector on the other hand." He was forthright in admitting he should have known better, but explained that "when you are going home to sleep at night with your very passionate lover, and you are trying to help"—well, sometimes things happen.

There was much more of the same, enough to convince the hearing panel. Apparently almost misty-eyed, the panel concluded that Weiss had "neither besmirched nor undermined the integrity of the legal profession."

Now, a layperson might think that paying off cops to protect prostitution would smudge up the old legal profession, at least a little bit. But that's only because, without benefit of law school, it's very difficult to comprehend complex legal arguments (which is why we don't think nonlawyers should be involved in disciplining lawyers, by the way).

In this case, for example, the attorneys on the hearing panel clearly understood that Weiss was paying off the police *not* as a lawyer, but *as a lover*—and that's a big distinction.

In fairness, though, even some lawyers had trouble understanding why being in love with a hooker made it okay to pay off cops. The Office of Disciplinary Counsel apparently failed to follow that argument, and recommended that Weiss be disbarred. And there was a precedent for such disbarment: the case of my old schoolmate, Peter Stern.

Stern had also made an improper cash payment ($5,000), not to a cop, but to a union official. It was a single indiscretion in an otherwise exemplary career that included major civic, religious, and charitable contributions. Like Weiss, Stern had been a star witness for federal prosecutors; unlike Weiss, he had not been involved in arranging protection for prostitution or any other illicit activity.

Peter Stern had been disbarred.

But the disciplinary board rejected the Office of Disciplinary Counsel's disbarment recommendation for Weiss, because the board understood the fine intricacies of the law, and immediately saw how Stern's case was different.

Stern, the board said, had made "repeated efforts" at corruption (even though there was only one payoff) and had been motivated by greed. In contrast, the board found that Weiss's "acts were singular" (unfortunate phrasing, since "acts" is, in fact, plural), that he was a victim, and that his actions were not for profit. (The loan Weiss arranged for Cheryl at 24 percent interest was not discussed, but these are busy lawyers on the board, they can't get bogged down in every little detail.)

(*Suggestion for Cheryl B.:* If you ever decide to set up another massage parlor, put the start-up costs on your bank card, and what you save in interest will cover the cops.)

The other key distinction, apparently, was that Peter Stern had the poor judgment *not* to be involved with a hooker, and as a result, did not get the benefit of board findings such as the following in the Weiss case:

- That Weiss and Cheryl B. "shared a serious romantic involvement."
- That the lawyer's misconduct was the "result of an aberrant fatal attraction."
- That Weiss's actions were "induced by the extortionate practices of high-ranking Philadelphia police officers and his romantic relationship with a woman."

But having concluded that Weiss did it for love, the board ran smack into another bad precedent, a case where another Pennsylvania lawyer did something for love: An anonymous attorney had taken the bar exam for his wife (who had previously flunked twice). In that case, the board had suggested a three-year suspension, but the Supreme Court of Pennsylvania ordered disbarment.

How could the board say that helping your wife slip through the bar exam (the cheating husband finished thirty-sixth out of eighteen hundred examinees, by the way) was worse than helping your mistress corrupt a big-city police department? It couldn't—so it just blew by the inconvenient precedent, not even making a serious effort to justify the inconsistencies.

Another intricacy that the disciplinary board fully appreciated was that Joe Weiss was a prominent *player* in Philadelphia, not only a well-connected lawyer, but also a major political contributor, and a dependable fund-raiser for charities. His character witnesses included former District Attorney Edward G. Rendell and onetime Eagles owner Leonard Tose.

Indeed, the board found that even after Weiss made the payoffs, his "reputation in the community and the opinion of those with whom he associates professionally and socially has remained and is one of great respect for both his professional abilities and personal integrity."

Having established that, and having identified the police inspector and Cheryl B. as the *real* culprits, the board recommended that Weiss be suspended for four years (rather than disbarred), and that his suspension be *retroactive* to December 21, 1987 (the date Weiss said he stopped practicing).

The Supreme Court of Pennsylvania adopted the board's recommendation. It was the first and only time a Pennsylvania suspension has been made retroactive to a date chosen by the suspended attorney.

Who cares about those legal technicalities?

No one.

What people care about is how things worked out for Joe and Cheryl.

Well, there was a wedding.

Philadelphia Inquirer reporters Robin Clark and Daniel R. Biddle disclosed that while he was paying off police at the instigation of his insistent "lover," Joe Weiss got married—to someone else.

The *Inquirer* reporters also spoke with the woman Weiss had described as his "very passionate lover," and Cheryl offered a somewhat less starry-eyed picture of their relationship.

"A love affair? Come on!" she said. "I might have gone to bed with him once or twice. He didn't do it for love. He did it for greed. I wasn't anything to him but a piece of tail."

A piece of TAIL?!

Did Joe Weiss fabricate his heart-rending love story to escape professional punishment?

Absolutely not.

Because even if he did make up the story, the purpose of professional discipline, as we'll see, is not to punish.

Professional Courtesy

In the late 1980s, the American Bar Association turned its attention to lawyer discipline and discovered, surprisingly, that it was a little shorthanded.

As you'll recall, the ABA is a lawyers' union (or, in our view, a professional body) formed more than a century ago, for the same purpose as most trade unions: "to raise the economic and social status of lawyers." Our trade union has done better than most; indeed, with *average* attorney pay now over $100,000 per year, the ABA could give the AFL-CIO lessons.

Along the way, the ABA itself has also grown big and fat.

- With more than 300,000 attorney members, it's the largest professional group in the *world*. (Of course, signing up all those members is a little like shooting fish in a barrel, since two thirds of all the lawyers in the world are American lawyers to start.)

- It has an annual budget of more than $50 million, not big by Defense Department standards, but not bad for a voluntary, private organization either. ABA members qualify for a variety of bennies, including tax-deductible vacations (disguised as annual working meetings), usually in places like Honolulu or New Orleans rather than Des Moines or Newark; rental car discounts; and group life insurance.

- The ABA churns out more propaganda than Tass and Tammy Faye Bakker combined, and it's a slick, multimedia effort, mountains of books and pamphlets, cassettes and videotapes. The legal profession is the basic topic, but a quick survey of titles shows that this covers a lot of ground.

  The *Animal Law Report,* for example, is near the top of the list; there is no clue whether this is monkeys-have-rights-too, or how-to-maximize-damages-in-dog-bite-cases. *Arson for Profit,* which sounds like a matchbook-cover career plan, occurs a few entries later, far enough from *Reusing Old Buildings* that no one gets any ideas. Then there's a handful of practical how-to works (*How to Survive the First Year of Law School,* for example, and for those who make it out of law school into the Club, the always popular *How to Avoid Being Sued by Your Client*), some patriotic titles (*Blessings of Liberty*), and even some whimsical ones (*Rubber Stamps Can Make an Impression*).

In general, the ABA works with the efficiency you would expect from an organization composed of a few hundred thousand lawyers. It has over a hundred committees, sections, task forces, and the like, which offer limitless opportunities for hearings, debates, meetings and reports, with very little risk of any decisive action being taken.

In 1988, someone noticed that it had been more than twenty years since the ABA had taken a serious look at lawyer discipline. At the same time, the ABA recognized an ominous number of challenges to the legal profession's historic self-regulation. The Securities and Exchange Commission and the Federal Trade Commission had both taken tentative jabs at the legal monopoly, and in a few states, there was even talk of regulating lawyers just like hairdressers and funeral directors.

Zounds!

Time to get serious about lawyer discipline. An ABA planning group thought that a national evaluation of lawyer disciplinary systems might be the answer—but who should make that evaluation?

Well, remember old ABA president Eugene Thomas ("we are the best-disciplined profession in the world")?

He had anticipated this sort of issue a couple of years before, when he reassured everyone that concerns about ethics and professional discipline would be handled by the ABA committees. So the planners flipped open the ABA organizational chart, and found plenty of possibilities:

- Standing Committee on Professional Discipline
- Standing Committee on Ethics and Professional Responsibility
- Standing Committee on Lawyers' Responsibility for Client Protection
- Special Coordinating Committee on Professionalism
- Standing Committee on Lawyer Competence
- Various other committees and subcommittees of sections and divisions, which, like the above groups, were already involved in the areas of lawyer discipline or competence.

But there was a problem.

The committees, unfortunately, were all busy.

Actually, the ABA planning group did not state it quite that way. Here's what it said:

Each of these committees has an ongoing and full agenda of projects and programs to implement ABA policy and goals within its area of jurisdiction. To undertake a review of national scope of the self-regulatory mechanisms of the profession would require an existing ABA unit to suspend its other activities for at least two years. To do so would destroy the continuity and momentum of ongoing programs. Expertise of committee members and staff would be lost in those ongoing operations.

Busy, busy.

And even if one of those committees did have a little spare time, the ABA planning group did not think any of them would be right for the task.

"No existing ABA unit," the group concluded, "can objectively conduct the nationwide evaluation" of lawyer disciplinary systems.

Now a cynic might conclude that any professional group with 300,000-plus members and over a hundred committees that cannot come up with anyone to look at lawyer discipline is not too interested in discipline.

But let's not be cynical.

I've never made it to the committee sessions or even to the annual working meetings, but as an ABA member in good standing (last time I checked), I have a pretty good idea how an ABA evaluation of lawyer disciplinary systems might come out. And with the ABA committees all tied up right now, I've got a little spare time, so let's take a look at what happens when lawyers break the lawyer rules.

And even though the ABA did not give me permission to reprint the Secret Rules, and ABA publications always warn "Copyright—All Rights Reserved" (even on uncreative items, such as pages of statistics compiled from public records), we'll turn the other cheek and do the opposite: No Rights Reserved.

If the ABA would like to pirate the following as its

"National Evaluation of Lawyer Disciplinary Systems" (since all those committees are busy, it could be a couple of years before they get around to it), that's okay.

Harold Casety took some Bentyl tablets, some sleeping pills, and drank about half a gallon of wine. Then he got into a bitter argument with his girlfriend, which ended when he pumped five bullets into her body.

He turned himself in. After pleading guilty to manslaughter, he was sentenced to six years in prison, and served more than three years before he was paroled.

That was in California.

Harold Casety was a lawyer. Putting five slugs into his girlfriend did not change that, and indeed, the whole time he was making license plates or taking transcendental meditation or whatever they do in the California slammer, attorney Casety remained in professional good standing—in Florida and Pennsylvania.

Maintaining his license to practice from the penitentiary, Casety discovered, was no more complicated than keeping his driver's license current. He simply had a friend mail in his annual registration fee, using the friend's office as his Pennsylvania business address.

When they finally figured this out, after Casety was out on parole, the lawyer disciplinarians were not amused. Casety was eventually suspended in Florida and disbarred in Pennsylvania. Ironically, though, Casety's Pennsylvania disbarment was not for blowing away his girlfriend, but for failing to do the paperwork required of lawyers who kill girlfriends: An attorney convicted of a serious crime is required to notify the Pennsylvania board within twenty days of sentencing. (And this requirement, the Supreme Court of Pennsylvania noted with unintended acuity, "applied to all Pennsylvania lawyers, whether they were in prison or out of prison.")

But even though Casety was disbarred, his case is a

handy jumping-off point for an evaluation of lawyer discipline, because it exposes a major loophole in the system.

It's not one system.

It's *fifty* systems.

The reason a lawyer can be—simultaneously—sitting in prison in the Golden State and in good standing in the Sunshine State is that each state has its own lawyer disciplinary system. They're all different, of course, because any uniform set of rules might undermine the delicate balance of federalism, which is another way of saying it might force all lawyers to meet some minimum standard of professional conduct.

Knowing the game, Bad Lawyers can hopscotch around the country until they land on a friendly location—or at least find a place to practice where no one has heard about their prior misdeeds. Like the old American frontier, the profession still promises redemption, giving a fellow who has made a bad mistake the chance to move on to a new town and get a fresh start.

But wouldn't the new clients quickly hear about their lawyer's bad old reputation?

No.

There's no easy way to find out, because lawyers generally oppose the idea of a national computer index detailing professional misconduct. (And, believe it or not, as we'll see, clients who spread the word about Bad Lawyers can, in many states, be tossed into jail.) But lawyer opposition to the idea of creating national professional disciplinary records is not inflexible. Indeed, Congress, brimming full of lawyers, recently decided it *would* be a good idea to have a national data bank detailing professional discipline imposed—in the *medical* profession.

As a result, a cardiologist fired from a Boston hospital because he just couldn't seem to find all those pesky sponges after the operation is going to have a tough time finding hospital work in Chicago or San Diego—or anywhere. By federal law, it's all in the national computer: doctor discipline, the outcome of medical malpractice cases (including out-of-court settlements), even adverse actions taken by local medical societies in the peer review process.

Obviously, we can't let Bad Doctors run loose.

But lawyers . . . well, that's a little more complicated. We have a duty to maintain public confidence in the legal system, and also to be sure minor mistakes do not unfairly tarnish attorney reputations. Mindful of these concerns, the ABA's National Discipline Data Bank is somewhat more, ah, responsible, than its medical counterpart (after all, we don't usually deal with life-and-death issues).

In the first place, the ABA data bank is limited to *public* discipline, so it does not pick up the hundreds of misbehaving lawyers who receive private professional scoldings. Also, since depositing data in the ABA bank is voluntary, no one knows how complete it is, and in any event, it lags years behind the crimes.

How many years? Florida lawyer Peter T. Roman, whom we met earlier, was not disbarred until *eight years* after he filed a forged document with the court to rip off a client's estate. That's a little extreme. His Sunshine State colleague, Edward Pedrero, disbarred for his role in a drug-importing scheme *five years* after he began supplying phony documents for the dealers, was more typical.

Finally, no matter how egregious, malpractice verdicts against lawyers and crimes committed by lawyers do not make the ABA printout at all, unless professional discipline results (which is why attorney Casety was still in good standing in jail, until he got behind in his paperwork).

Despite the ABA data bank, then, the odds of a Bad Lawyer successfully slipping back into practice in a new state after a brush with professional discipline are a lot better than, say, your getting away with a purchase ten dollars over your Visa card credit limit.

Some lawyers don't even bother to make a run for the border. Disbarred attorney David Azrak, for one, was recently charged with practicing law—and stealing more than $37,000 from client personal injury recoveries—in the *same* state that had yanked his ticket just a year earlier. This is a tricky problem, since short of branding their foreheads with a big scarlet "D," how is anyone supposed to distinguish disbarred lawyers from the real thing?

(Indeed, some lawyers don't even let jail interfere with their practice. Florida lawyer Stephen Terrill Lee, in the lockup on a cocaine rap, told the *National Law Journal* that "in prison, people told me I was crazy not to be practicing—that guys did it all the time by mail.")

The other threshold observation about lawyer disciplinary systems is that, while they come in fifty varieties, they all have one feature in common. And, by coincidence, it's one we're already familiar with from the ABA: They're all a little shorthanded.

The fifty state disciplinary agencies employ, *in total,* fewer than 300 full-time staff lawyers. Add the investigators and paralegals, clerks and secretaries, and the national total is still less than 1,000 disciplinary staffers. Even the states with big boards are shorthanded; California, for example, has over 60 disciplinary staff attorneys, but it also has over 100,000 lawyers, and their practice provokes more than 20,000 complaints annually.

If you were wondering how a couple of reporters from the *Philadelphia Inquirer,* without subpoenas, access to secret records, or power to make deals on discipline, could have discovered that Joe Weiss—supposedly in mid-passion—married someone other than his paramour, while the official Dobermans on the state disciplinary board missed it, here's the answer: The *Inquirer* has a lot more staffers than the disciplinary board does.

Not surprisingly, the shorthanded lawyer disciplinary boards are also a little short on cash. There's an excellent reason for this: In most states, the expenses of lawyer discipline are paid by lawyers (one of the few drawbacks of self-regulation). We want to do what's right, of course, but there's no point in paying for a Mercedes if a Honda will get us there; the average state budget for lawyer discipline comes in at a frugal fifty dollars per lawyer. (Keep in mind that these disciplinary boards are trying to catch *us*—did someone think we should buy them nuclear weapons?!)

Now, even if the ABA was doing this evaluation, it would probably be forced to concede that our lawyer disciplinary systems are stretched pretty thin. In fact, four states (California, New York, Texas, and Pennsylvania) have nearly half of all the lawyers employed in the discipline business, and most other states have fewer professional enforcers than you have fingers on one hand.

Against . . . about 850,000 lawyers.

That's how many lawyers are moving around out there (not even counting the disbarred ones trying to sneak back into the game). With those numbers, enforcing lawyer ethical rules would seem to be impossible, just too few cops chasing too many robbers.

At best, the enforcers might be able to do about what NBA refs do, shut down the really rough stuff, nail lawyers like Casety who kill people, hit the biggest attorney embezzlers and druggies, and hope that deters the others. But three hundred lawyer-zebras are not going to stop every little attorney trick inside, no point in even trying, might as well just let the lawyers play.

But what about *self*-regulation?

Don't the disciplinarians get a lot of professional help, since the Secret Rules say lawyers are all supposed to call their own fouls whenever they see them?

That's a common misconception, probably resulting from the fact that there *is* an ethical rule for lawyers called "Reporting Professional Misconduct." But what Rule 8.3 actually says is that a lawyer having "**knowledge**" that another lawyer has committed an ethical violation that raises a "**substantial**" question about the lawyer's honesty, trustworthiness, or "**fitness as a lawyer**" shall inform appropriate authorities.

With the Weasel Words highlighted, it should be easy to see why Rule 8.3 has not set off a din of whistle-blowing in the legal profession.

Take, for example, the case of New Jersey lawyer Louis J. Nitti. Colleagues may well have wondered, over drinks, how Lou could afford so many gambling trips to Atlantic City, but they certainly did not have "**knowledge**" that he had grabbed $164,000 from client trust funds—until he confessed. There was nothing to report, rumors and suspicions don't count, and—as we've seen—knowledge is something that lawyers are expert at *not* having.

Even in the few cases where a lawyer actually has knowledge, how big does a question have to be to qualify as "**substantial**"?

It must be a "**material**" matter of "**clear**" and "**weighty**" importance, according to the Rules; we're talking big crimes here, maybe not quite Nuremberg level, but right up there—the appropriate authorities can't be bothered with every little slipup and indiscretion.

Like attorney Frick chasing after Peggy what's-her-name.

Sure, the courthouse crowd in Kirksville, Missouri, probably "**knew**" that old Bill Frick was making a fool of himself with that young client, but if he had a problem, folks figured, it was with his hormones, not his fitness as a lawyer, certainly not any "**substantial**" question about that. How could there be, when—even after it all came out, the dirty letters, crazy threats, shooting and all—sixty-eight lawyers were willing to stand up as character witnesses at Frick's disbarment?

Once you work through the Weasel Words, then, it's clear that the rule called "Reporting Professional Misconduct" actually contains a number of good reasons not to.

Moreover, lawyers don't like snitches to start with, and nothing in the rule provides any incentive to become one. Indeed, when practitioners encounter professional misconduct, the overwhelming majority of them follow a rule somewhat less complicated than Rule 8.3:

Mum's the word.

"Probably no other professional requirement is as widely ignored by lawyers subject to it," asserts Charles W. Wolfram, author of *Modern Legal Ethics*. "Lawyer complaints form a relatively small percentage of the complaints received by lawyer discipline agencies."

Another legal scholar, Ronald D. Rotunda, states flatly: "Lawyers rarely report other lawyers."

Critics may call that irresponsible, proof that self-regulation does not work.

We call it professional courtesy.

Almost 80 percent say lawyers have a negative public image.

That's obviously a skewed sample of lawyer-bashers trying to smear the legal profession, we immediately suspect, certainly not the view of the public at large.

And in fact, the suspicion is half right. The sample is *not* representative of the general public—good news—but hold the champagne, barristers, because it turns out that the respondents were not lawyer haters, but rather, lawyers.

But while four out of five lawyers think lawyers have a negative image, two out of three—according to the same survey, recently published in the *ABA Journal*—say we don't deserve it. (If your attorney acts even more surly than you have come to expect, these two responses may explain why: We know you don't like us, and we don't think it's fair.)

How would lawyers spruce up this bad image we don't deserve?

About half would do it with PR of one sort or another

(43 per cent say increase education of the public by bar associations; another 9 percent suggest hiring a public relations consultant to do a media campaign), while 27.2 percent recommend improving attorney discipline systems.

Coincidentally, this result mirrors the statement of the ABA planning group that, nearly two years before, decided it was a good idea to look at lawyer discipline but found that all of its committees were busy.

"A nationwide evaluation of disciplinary systems is needed," the ABA panel said, "to determine if the existing disciplinary mechanisms have failed to gain credibility with the public, and if so, whether the failure is due to poor performance or poor public relations."

We're on to something here.

Maybe our evaluation of lawyer disciplinary systems can be boiled down to a single question:

Does the legal profession have bad discipline or lousy PR?

Assume, just for argument, that the only problem is ineffective public relations. That should be easy to fix. All we need to do is identify the big issues where the public has a distorted picture, and then develop some positive themes to get our side across.

Let's see how it might work.

Public misperception number 1. Lawyers try to hush up professional misconduct.

That misunderstanding, of course, flows from our fondness for secrecy. In most states, all disciplinary proceedings are confidential, even after formal charges. In a handful of states, even after they have been disbarred or suspended, lawyers are not required to notify their clients. And in roughly half the states, under so-called gag rules, clients can be *jailed* for contempt of court if they discuss charges they have filed against a lawyer—unless the charges result in public discipline. (That's one way to put a stop to irresponsible client bad-mouthing.)

* * *

PR strategy: Simply tell the truth, show why secrecy is vital to the profession, using some respected authority. The Supreme Court of Pennsylvania, for example, explained: "As a primary objective of . . . [discipline] is the rehabilitation of the lawyer (in addition, of course, to the protection of the public interest), confidentiality may be considered essential to ensure that rehabilitative efforts are not thwarted by disclosures that may be prejudicial."

On second thought, maybe we should use a *symbolic* approach, something more subtle. We could pick a theme like "Silence is Golden," show worshipers in church or peaceful country landscapes or something, with the tag line "Sponsored by the ABA."

This pitch probably needs some work.

Public misperception number 2. Lawyers who get convicted on felony charges should be automatically disbarred.

This simplistic public view has some surface appeal, but that's because the fundamental constitutional rights of lawyers have been overlooked. A media campaign could definitely help here.

PR strategy: Theme: "Raw Deal."

Hammer home the idea that lawyers battle to protect the rights of every other occupational group to a fair hearing before their professional licenses are lifted . . . but when it comes to our own profession, some people think the ultimate punishment should be automatic, with no hearing at all.

The visuals for this should have a strong civil rights/fairness focus, maybe pick up on the idea of Brave Man Against the Mob.

Another major argument against automatic disbarment of lawyer-felons is the concern that innocent lawyers might plead guilty to misdemeanors, fearing that if they don't, they could be charged with felonies and lose their license to practice. (Honest—a law professor actually wrote that in a respected law review.)

Powerful stuff, but we're probably going to need an agency with a strong creative staff to get it across.

Public misconception number 3. Even in the rare cases where lawyers get disciplined, there are endless delays before it happens.

PR strategy: We have a blockbuster to turn this misperception around. It's a real case, with drugs, sex, violence, it'll compete with the soaps *and* the cop shows, grade school kids will be forming fan clubs for the lawyer disciplinary board.

Theme: "The Mounties Always Get Their Man—California-style."

The spot opens with Bernie waking up at 5:00 A.M., still high on drugs. He sees his teenage friends Vicki and Peter naked on a mattress in the living room. Segue into a drug-hazed flashback . . . I ordered Vicki out yesterday . . . and she's still there . . . where's that gun? Bam! Bam! The shots don't kill Peter instantly, but Bernie drags the body into the hall. Fade as the police arrive, with Bernie explaining that the now dead Peter had tried to break in.

The chase begins.

Five years slip by.

Cut to the California hearing panel, considering the professional discipline case of lawyer Bernard Sabbath Strick, previously convicted of manslaughter, and drug and weapons offenses.

Relentlessly, the disciplinarians continue on the trail.

Another year passes.

Dramatic cut to the public hearing on Strick's recommended discipline, being conducted by the California Bar Review Department.

Now they're almost close enough to grab him.

Two more years elapse.

They get him!

Climax with trumpet fanfare.

It took eight years, but the determined disciplinarians never wavered, and Bernard Strick was finally disbarred.

On reflection, maybe it's more than PR; perhaps there *are* some flaws in the lawyer disciplinary systems.

Let's recap the evidence so far.

- There are more than fifty lawyer disciplinary boards in this country, all with different rules, and all operating mostly in secret.
- Unlike the medical profession, we have no comprehensive national listing of lawyer discipline actions and malpractice verdicts, and the various disciplinary boards often don't talk to each other.
- The disciplinary boards are understaffed and underfunded, and lawyers almost universally ignore their professional duty to report misconduct by their colleagues.

Those sound like fairly serious defects, but it's really impossible to reach a final judgment—as lawyers will recognize—prior to answering a basic question:

What is the *purpose* of lawyer discipline?

Now, we've saved a little surprise for the end here, so it's important to follow closely.

The purpose of lawyer discipline is *not* to punish the lawyer.

That's right.

Indeed, it's one of the great historical principles of the law, derived from a famous 1778 case that set forth the objective of attorney discipline. "It is *not by way of punishment*," the revered Lord Mansfield wrote, "but the court on such cases, exercise their discretion, whether a man whom they have formerly admitted, is a proper person to be continued on the roll or not."

Over the next couple of centuries, Mansfield's gobbledygook about continuing on the roll has not gotten too much attention, but his inspired idea that the purpose of discipline is not to punish has become a treasured tenet in the legal catechism, repeated by courts in hundreds of discipline cases.

"The purpose of these proceedings is not to punish the attorney," a typical opinion states. "Rather, the primary goal is protection of the public and the legal profession."

That sounds reasonable, if you don't think too hard about it, and it certainly gives the legal profession some leeway in dealing with Bad Lawyers. And even though the notion that it's-not-for-punishment runs directly contrary to our experience with discipline in every other area—from the nun whacking your knuckles to the boss docking your pay to the highway patrolman slapping you with a ticket—the amazing part is that no one seems to have taken serious issue with this blatantly bogus concept.

Oh, well.

Who are we to quarrel with over two hundred years of legal history?

If punishment is not the purpose of discipline, we would have to conclude that—despite the flaws we've noted—our lawyer disciplinary systems are doing a bang-up job.

They're second to none when it comes to not punishing.

Just a professional courtesy.

Guess Whose Fault?

Who—or what—is to blame for lawyer misconduct? If we rule out genetic flaws, television, dietary deficiencies, and God (don't laugh, the Almighty is always high on our list of likely culprits when bad things happen that we didn't anticipate; check out the "Acts of God" clause in any contract), then the list of potential suspects is pretty short: It could be lawyers, clients, or the legal system.

And since we've just concluded that the legal system—or at least the disciplinary part of it—is performing as intended, that leaves only lawyers or clients, which would seem to make the choice easy: Blame the lawyers.

Clients, after all, are overwhelmingly the *victims* of attorney misconduct, even lawyers will not argue about that. In nearly every state, lawyers are forced to ante up a few bucks for something called the Client Security Fund, which is a pot of money used to repay clients after Bad Lawyers steal their money. Obviously, we wouldn't have signed up for any program like that unless we thought there were enough client-victims out there to be a potential problem.

Even so, it would be a mistake to be too hasty here.

In the first place, it should be clear by now that the concept of "victim" can take some funny bounces when lawyers are in the game. More important, who says that victims cannot be to blame for what happens to them? As lawyers, we regularly argue the opposite, especially—remember Jack Litman in the Preppie Murder case—when we're trying to get a live client off the hook for killing a dead victim.

Moreover, astonishing as it may seem, given the constant criticism of lawyers, the role of *clients* in the profession has received virtually no critical scrutiny. As new lawyers are often surprised to discover, clients are not bit players in the legal business; they're what it's all about. Still, there are lots of critical reviews for lawyers, but no complaints about clients, not even any quibbles.

Obviously, that's because most of the complainers about lawyers *are* clients, so it's not surprising that they don't blame themselves. And lawyers don't usually shoot back, since for most, expressing true feelings about clients would be bad for business. When a lawyer next speaks at the Kiwanis Club, you can bet your lunch that the aggravation of constantly having to kowtow to clients will *not* be among his themes.

Indeed, when you glance through your lawyer's slick new marketing brochure, you'll find the opposite message: "We value our many clients, and welcome the challenge of working with each of them in today's increasingly complex legal environment," blah, blah, blah.

Don't believe it.

Clients all have problems. If they didn't, they wouldn't need to pay out good money for the privilege of being clients. That means if a lawyer has a lot of clients, he has a lot of problems—their problems. And while lawyers in private practice learn to tolerate this reality in the interest of buying groceries, the plain fact is that most attorneys don't really like problems any more than anyone else does.

Wait—that can't be right.

Why would anyone become a lawyer in the first place if he did not want to grapple with thorny legal problems for clients?

Well, amazing as it sounds, many lawyers do not fully understand the part clients play in the law business until sometime *after* they have invested $50,000 or $75,000 in a legal education. And then it's a little late.

That's because law school problems don't involve flesh-and-blood clients—or at least, I don't remember any. Instead, looking back, I recall complex abstractions and kaleidoscopic bits and pieces, like Professor Charles Fried (later Solicitor General Fried) telling our criminal law class that the only *real* cure for chronic criminal behavior is old age; for some reason, that odd insight stuck.

Then there was Professor Louis Loss, nationally respected guru of the Securities and Exchange Commission laws, drumming home the basic concept of agency law ("*anything* you can do can be done by your agent—you can *live* and *breathe* through an agent, provided he's *authorized*"); and of course, the legendary Professor Casner, who gave me a borderline grade in Property, probably deserved, since all I remember from the course is that the rule against perpetuities has something to do with twenty-one years plus a life in being. (Whatever that may mean, it has not—happily—come up in practice since.)

The professors had crackling intellectual firepower; exchanges with them were intimidating and intense; their legal puzzles were abstract, challenging, and fun.

But nothing about clients.

Still, we shouldn't make too much of this, because students in law school are supposed to be smart. Who did we think was going to pay us money to solve legal problems, Santa Claus?

Once out of the sanctuary of academe, in any event, lawyers quickly learn the central fact of life in the law business:

CLIENTS.

Careerwise, clients are make or break.

Without John T. Scopes and Eugene V. Debs, Clarence Darrow would still have been a brilliant lawyer, but you would never have heard of him.

And *with* clients, especially clients who will stick with a lawyer no matter which firm he works for ("transportable business," we call them in the trade), lawyers are transformed into "rainmakers," and can jump from firm to firm, looking for the richest deal.

"It's like baseball," said Washington, D.C., lawyer headhunter Jonathan Spivak, "you go where the money is." Some older practitioners wince at this, remembering the genteel old days when law partners were, without question and without regard to economic happenstance, partners for life—even in those less productive later years.

No longer.

"The person we're moving today is a rainmaker bringing in between $1 million and $5 million," a legal search executive recently told the *Philadelphia Inquirer* (sounding not unlike someone talking about moving Ford Tempos or refrigerators or color TVs).

So the name of the game is clients, and that's also where the trouble starts.

John Roper was a client.

He was the one that lawyer Paul I. Mostman wanted a hit man to kill.

Taking a closer look at the Mostman-Roper relationship, it's somewhat more understandable why the California disciplinary board and Supreme Court were so sympathetic to the attorney. (Mostman, as you'll recall, received only a two-year suspension.)

Early in their acquaintance, Roper told Mostman that he was the local Godfather's nephew, and said he worked as an organized-crime hit man. That did not trouble Mostman initially; there's no law that says hit men can't have lawyers, and indeed, they have a high likelihood of needing them.

So Mostman did Roper's personal injury work, and also handled a couple of disputes with his neighbors. Roper liked the results enough to refer some friends to Mostman for legal work, even introducing himself as the lawyer's "partner" to one of them. Then Roper started preparing legal documents on Mostman's letterhead. The first indication that the relationship was heading south came when Mostman took exception to some of Roper's "legal work," and threatened to go to the police. Roper replied that, if he did, the lawyer might "find [his] little girl hanging from a tree."

Suddenly, Mostman had an incredible run of bad luck with cars, in each case while parked in his assigned space in his building's secured parking lot. The paint on his newly restored Italia was intentionally scraped with a sharp object. His mother's Chevy, which he used while the Italia was being fixed, had its antenna snapped in half. Ditto the antenna on Mostman's Mazda, which he used while the Chevy was out. Trading up (and apparently still not getting it), Mostman drove his open-top Ferrari to the office, and, after a hard day of lawyering, returned to find that someone had dumped feces on the front seat.

At this point, it's pretty obvious what most lawyers would have done: slap the operators of the supposedly secure parking lot with a large lawsuit. But Mostman, as we know, had a different legal strategy. Convinced that his client was behind it all (and his car problems escalated further, with fatal potential, when someone removed all but one lug nut on one of his wheels), Mostman decided to hire a hit man to hit the hit man.

An extreme case, obviously.

But it makes a point.

Clients are wildly unpredictable, and can even be dangerous to the lawyer. Most, of course, do not provoke the old barrister to violence. But they do provide plenty of potential for getting lawyers in trouble, and the dangers arise mainly in two basic areas:

Getting clients—and keeping them.

How do we get clients? Back in Clarence Darrow's day, the answer would have been simple: Be an excellent lawyer.

When a lawyer won cases, small ones at first, his happy clients would tell their friends, who would engage him for larger cases; people would hear about that, the word would spread, and pretty soon he would have plenty of clients.

It's usually a little more complicated today, but that's how it worked for plaintiff's lawyer J. Michael Liles—sort of. Liles represented two clients who were suing a large company. As a result of his aggressive work in those cases, his abilities came to the attention of Playtex Corp., which then signed Liles up, according to *The Washington Post*, for a $500,000 consulting deal.

The only problem was that Liles then had to withdraw from the two cases he had brought for his original clients, since the large company they were suing, for toxic shock syndrome, was—you guessed it—Playtex. (Oh, and Playtex did not make the cushy offer until *after* Liles had gotten damaging documents from its files, in the course of discovery on behalf of the two clients he later dropped.)

Ethical?

The Playtex insurance carrier didn't think so, refused to pay any part of the $500,000, and was quoted in the *Post* as being "concerned by the ethical considerations and the long-term ramifications of an agreement of this nature."

Liles, however, told the reporter that he had wanted to be sure he did not do anything unethical, and so had sought out some objective opinions before making the Playtex deal; everyone he'd asked had said the deal was fine.

Who had he consulted?

Several lawyers and judges.

Oh. Actually, that makes sense, because lawyers and judges know how tough it is to get clients today; even Clarence Darrow might have trouble, because a couple of key things have changed.

First, the competition. There are *hundreds of thousands* of lawyers in that legal jungle out there, *all* fighting for clients; Clarence never had to contend with anything like that. Check out the yellow pages: If your city is like mine, lawyers are the biggest single category of advertisers, even pushing ahead of the used car guys (and with comparably tasteful ads).

Second, what lawyers do has changed. Only a small minority spend any time in courtrooms—and when you're sitting behind a desk, say, revising a lease, it's tough to make client-winning drama out of that. Plus, even if you *are* a superstar desk lawyer, in an age of scanners and word processors, whatever brilliance you added to the last deal will be in the standard form of every hack lawyer in town on the next deal.

In short, we hate to admit it, but a lot of what we do, especially if it involves legal documents, is—dirty word—*fungible*. When it comes to the quality of advice and judgment, you can still find a world of difference between lawyers, but if it's only a matter of documents, well, comparable firms will churn out comparable paper. (Indeed, as Rosemary Furman proved, doing the documents competently does not always even require a law degree.)

There's one more serious complication in getting clients: We're not allowed to ask.

"Solicitation" has been a longtime no-no in the legal profession, indeed, one of the most serious offenses. An early version of the Secret Rules required any lawyer hearing that a lawyer had solicited a client "immediately to inform thereof, to the end that the offender may be disbarred." (Odd, when you consider the bad stuff we wink at; maybe we're a little touchy about being compared to that *other* profession in the solicitation business.)

More recently, the prohibition has been modified to permit advertising by lawyers, but lawyers are still barred from directly soliciting clients (except for relatives and close friends).

Whatever the reasons for the ban (which we suspect had something to do with the lawyers who wrote the rule wanting to keep the clients they had), the result of it has *not* been to eliminate the unseemly pursuit of clients by attorneys. Instead, it has simply driven all of the action underground, creating a maze of tricks tailored to feed each legal specialty.

So how *do* we get clients?

- Personal injury lawyers, who take a lot of heat in this area, have graduated from chasing ambulances. Exhibit A: *The Wall Street Journal* reported that, when a Texas department store roof collapsed, some PI lawyers had runners on the scene dressed up like Red Cross workers, digging victims out and signing them up at the same time; at a Detroit plane crash, a runner was disguised as a priest.
- Criminal defense lawyers sometimes have deals with cops, since they regularly have dealings with criminals.
- Direct mail is another technique, and it's not limited to plaintiff's lawyers. Cadwalader, Wickersham and Taft, blue-chip Big Firm, chummed around for clients with a direct-mail piece touting its inside connections in Washington.
- Big firms generally, though, favor lavish entertainment as a way to lure future clients, hosting everything from Super Bowl galas to racetrack parties.

- And sometimes, lawyers try to get future clients by pulling their punches in cases involving current clients. Most lawyers don't see anything improper about that, of course; it's just a professional accommodation. For instance, attorneys agree every day to extensions of time for the other side to file a pleading, not because it's justified, but in the hope of a future client referral from the opposing lawyer (or, at least, comparable consideration the next time *we* are late with a pleading).

  Of course, current clients would almost never agree to that.

  But who asks?

Hard as it is, however, getting clients is the easy part of the problem.

What clients ask us to do is often much more difficult.

In the first place, all clients want all legal tasks done *now*.

In some situations, that is understandable: The criminal defendant who uses his only phone call to reach his lawyer at 3:00 A.M. is not interested in hearing that the mouthpiece might be able to spring him a week from Thursday.

He wants out *now*.

The battered spouse who finally gets up the courage to file for divorce does not want to spend one more second with that monster.

She needs those pleadings filed *now*.

The widow in the nursing home who has finally decided to put Charles back in the will, but wants to cut Margaret out again, may *not* be in any huge rush to see the lawyer. But she may get visits from Charles or Margaret, who have their own ideas about who Grandma's lawyer should be—or she may die before Charles gets written back into the will, in which case the lawyer gets sued by Charles.

Head for the nursing home.

Even legal work that would seem more leisurely usually is not. Executives buying and selling companies want agreements done now—markets change, interest rates move, sellers decide not to, the imperative is to get the deal *done*. Complex lawsuits may seem to move like molasses, but the lawyers who litigate them spend those years running for airplanes to get to depositions, staying up all night preparing pleadings, rushing to court to argue motions.

Law, in short, is a service business (another detail that does not get a lot of attention in law school), and every client views his problem as urgent.

But if each client's concern is a crisis, some lawyers figure, then no client's emergency is really too pressing. The result is that the most common cause of lawyer discipline is not fraud or embezzlement, not drug abuse or even incompetence—but *general neglect*.

Translation for clients: We're tired of hearing about your problem, you're wearing us out.

What does "general neglect" mean in everyday practice?

It means that your lawyer refuses to return your phone calls, or doesn't get around to tracking down those witnesses until it's too late to find them.

In extreme cases, it can mean that your lawyer does not file your lawsuit until it's too late, after the statute of limitations has run out, which will cause you to lose your rights—forever.

Lawyer misconduct, then, is really the lawyer's fault.

Or is it?

After all, when I'm not taking your call, it's because some other client has me tied up on the other line, maybe screaming at me from some federal prison, or complaining about a fee. When your divorce complaint doesn't get filed, it's not because the lawyer is playing golf; more often, it means that another client's complaint *is* getting filed.

We're not trying to shift the blame, of course, but . . .

Peter Stern told it like it is, describing what his client

said before the payment that got Stern disbarred: "Well, they [the client] cast around for something to do and in a discussion with me, they said, if you can't help us . . . and we're paying you this retainer, and more than the retainer sometimes, we are going to have to take another tack. We are going to have to do something else. There was discussion about—I don't remember the words or the give and take, but they said something to the effect, we want to see if paying him [the union official] softens his attitude."

Not that we're trying to excuse the lawyer . . . but doesn't that part about the retainer sound almost like blackmail?

At a minimum, the payoff was a dumb, illegal, stupid thing to do—and guess whose idea?

The client's.

Elizabeth Ann Duke was a dream client.

An underground revolutionary, Duke became a fugitive from justice rather than show up at a preliminary hearing, thereby giving her lawyer, Linda Backiel, the chance to go to jail for her client.

Identified by the FBI as a member of the revolutionary May 19 Movement, Duke had been indicted in 1985 after the discovery of a secret arsenal of military weapons and explosives. Two days before the hearing, she skipped.

Backiel, a frequent defender of radical opponents of American policy, was eventually subpoenaed to appear before the federal grand jury probing her client's disappearance. She refused, declaring that to appear would be "a betrayal of the client's trust," and "a subversion of the adversary system of justice." In 1990, the U.S. Third Circuit Court of Appeals ordered her to testify or be jailed for contempt; at this writing, she has not testified.

Backiel's political views might be somewhere out on the far left fringe, but her willingness to go to jail for her client puts her squarely in the mainstream of the American legal profession. Believe it or not, most lawyers would *welcome* the opportunity to defend the sacred constitutional rights of clients against tyrannical government forces, even going to prison if that's what it takes (although we don't relish that hard time quite so much as we get older and softer).

It's a secret lawyer fantasy.

Indeed, right up there in the front lines of volunteers happy to go to jail for clients are the drug lawyers, not always viewed as paragons of principle. Actually, their stand is *not* one of pure principle; it also has to do with cash, specifically whether drug cash can be used to pay legal fees. The issue comes up in response to a new IRS policy demanding the names of all clients who pay cash fees over $10,000; drug lawyers contend that revealing those names would violate the attorney-client privilege, which makes it at least part-principle.

"I think there are hundreds of attorneys who will go to jail for this," a spokesman for the National Association of Criminal Defense Lawyers predicted, and while no one has yet spotted drug lawyers packing toothbrushes and lining up to get the cuffs on, the prospect of mass arrests seems to have stirred more enthusiasm than foreboding.

Again, the fantasy.

But here's the biggest part of our problem with clients: Going to jail to protect their precious rights is not what clients ask us to do. Instead, most times, the rights clients ask us to defend for them stop well this side of sacred. The hostile forces arrayed against our clients tend not to be harsh government inquisitors, but rather conniving former spouses, slippery business partners, tightfisted insurance companies, neighbors with loud dogs or encroaching trees or delinquent kids, or bill collectors. And the battles we fight for clients in daily practice almost never give us a chance to quote bravely from the Constitution as we're dragged off to the hoosegow.

For many lawyers, the reality of what legal work for clients actually involves is more than an unfulfilled fantasy, it's a fundamental career disappointment.

"Nobody ever calls me to say they're having a great year, or tell me they want to pay my fees," Miami lawyer Don Slesnick told *The Washington Post*. "They only call me when they're in trouble."

What do frustrated lawyers—or lawyers stressed out from trying to juggle conflicting client demands—do?

Allan McPeak, a Florida lawyer, watched nine close lawyer friends die before age fifty-five, two by suicide. He decided to leave the law and get a Ph.D. in counseling psychology.

Philadelphia lawyer Joe Moore, a respected litigator, decided to head for Wyoming and become a cowboy.

Greg Howard left a partnership at a large Minnesota firm to create the syndicated comic strip, *Sally Forth*.

Tom and Bonnie Menaker, both accomplished Pennsylvania lawyers, chucked their practices, sold the house, unloaded the plane, dumped the condo, and were last heard from setting sail on a world cruise on the boat where they plan to live permanently.

They didn't take any clients along.

Each year, something like forty thousand lawyers—roughly the same number that graduate from law school—make the same decision, and leave the legal profession.

But there is another solution, for lawyers who can figure out how to do it: A select few attorneys escape the frustrations of practice by becoming judges. The pay is low, compared to what most lawyers-turned-judges could have earned if they had continued to practice, and there are lots of problems on the bench.

But no clients.

Judge Not

Bugs.

In the ceiling.

No way.

A solid brick fortress with only one window, a thick slab of Thermopane framed by a burglar alarm, the building seemed totally secure from outside interference. In contrast to the nearby beauty parlors, pizza joints, and other shops, the business of the building did not seem to require making anyone feel at home: Its parking lot was surrounded by an eight-foot-high cyclone fence, topped by coils of shiny razor-barbed wire.

The building itself was apparently guarded by something equally potent, invisible but respected by local kids. It was mysteriously graffiti-free in a tough Philadelphia neighborhood full of aerosol art.

In fact, what protected the building was the violent reputation of the men who had built it as their headquarters, members of Roofers Local 30-30B, a union proud of its informal label: "Storm troopers of the building trades."

A decade earlier, nearly one thousand Roofers had overrun a nonunion work site at nearby Valley Forge, battering down fences, firebombing and vandalizing construction equipment—as hopelessly outnumbered Pennsylvania State Police simply watched. Roofer violence continued to make regular headlines in subsequent years, and for a time the bare-knuckled members of 30-30B seemed untouchable.

But then Roofer boss John McCullough—still a legendary bar-clearing tough guy at sixty—made a rare slip. It was Christmastime, and McCullough let the florist with two poinsettias walk right into his house, watched him place the flowers carefully on the kitchen table, and then it was too late when the man pulled out a .22 semiautomatic and pumped six shots into McCullough's head, killing him instantly as his wife watched.

When the FBI installed the bugs in union headquarters, the Roofer boss was McCullough's successor, Steve Traitz. A family man, Traitz did not drink, attended mass regularly, helped young men in trouble, supported charities generously, had lots of friends in high places, and could be moved to tears singing "God Bless America."

But like McCullough, Traitz did not get too misty-eyed about labor violence because, whether systematic or random, it was as basic to the roofing business as tar.

Roofing contractors suspected of bending work rules were routinely summoned to union headquarters, the FBI taps would reveal, where they were taken into the notorious "rubber room" and roughed up. Traitz acknowledged that his son, Joey, "comes in when they're gonna beat guys up," which meant his attendance was regular, and described a huge union goon admiringly as "beautiful . . . like a dog."

Even when there was no union issue involved, just a

barroom argument or sidewalk quarrel, Traitz knew—as did every area citizen who could comprehend a news bulletin—that his Roofers would, in his words, "punch you in the nose in a damn minute."

Knowing that, Traitz also knew that his men would be spending time in courtrooms. So he initiated a systematic—and secret—program to make certain that Philadelphia judges would give his guys a break. The program was not complicated: Traitz sent cash to judges.

Astonished FBI agents monitoring the microphones inside union headquarters heard him counting it out, going over with his messenger the list of judges to be paid. Deliveries would be made before Christmas, $200 to $500 per judge, cold cash in unmarked envelopes, no names outside, no greeting cards inside.

How would the judges recognize Santa?

Traitz's messenger, who not incidentally was the late John McCullough's first cousin, was a retired Philadelphia court officer. The judges all knew him. He had no problem getting to see any of them as he made his rounds to their chambers—this time tailed by FBI agents.

His deliveries complete, the messenger reported back to Traitz, who would not realize until a few days later that his career as Roofer boss, like John McCullough's, had been ended by a slipup at Christmastime.

Traitz discovered the FBI microphones on New Year's Eve.

"The roof leaked," he said into a microphone, shortly before the last one was ripped out. "Roof's leakin' like a mother."

But even if the FBI had not penetrated the scheme, it clearly would have come unraveled, since any judge finding that the envelope shoved into his hand was full of cash would certainly report it to the police.

Actually, none did that.

Or at least, given Local 30-30B's universally known

reputation for violence, the vast majority of judges would certainly refuse to accept Roofer cash.

Only one did that.

The other fifteen Philadelphia judges who received cash in plain envelopes from the Roofers' messenger took it—and told no one.

How does someone become a judge?

Like becoming a client, being named a judge does not require completion of any specialized training. Cops must get through the police academy, vets have to graduate from veterinary school, surgeons need a medical license. But dispensing justice must be something that comes naturally, because there is no Judge School, and no particular pedigree required.

Historically, judges did not even need a law degree. The Founding Fathers apparently thought justice was too important to trust to the lawyers, because in creating the United States Supreme Court, they did not require justices to have a legal education, or any other degree. The only constitutional requirement is that federal judges shall hold their office "during good behavior," and may be removed only by impeachment.

Over the years, however, the vast majority of American courts have come to require that judges have legal training, and the Supreme Court is now the distinct exception. So to become a judge, the first step is to be a lawyer.

Uhhh-oh.

Even if we don't admit it, there seem to be more than a few Bad Lawyers running loose among the attorney population. If the main credential for becoming a judge is to be a lawyer, no further testing or qualification required, what assurance is there that Bad Lawyers won't simply keep climbing up the career ladder, and turn into bad judges (or, more likely, the best judges money can buy)?

There are no guarantees. Indeed, there are not even

any huge obstacles between Bad Lawyers and black robes, because, despite a variety of judicial selection methods, it mostly comes down to knowing the right people.

In states that elect judges, the people that aspiring lawyers need to know are the political leaders and ward bosses. In making their acquaintance, cash is generally a welcome icebreaker. Veteran pols understand that intuitively, but some newcomers need to have it spelled out. This would seem to be a matter of some delicacy, and maybe it is, somewhere, but not in Philadelphia; unsqueamish political leaders there recently announced that any candidate for judge who wanted the Democratic endorsement should contribute $5,000 to the party.

Once that check clears, depending on its size, party bosses are in a better position to gauge a candidate's judicial temperament.

But where can a candidate for judge get that kind of money?

Not a problem.

The people who make their living in courtrooms are smart enough to invest in judges. Personal injury lawyers compete with insurance industry political action committees in showering campaign funds on judicial candidates. In Texas, attorneys representing Pennzoil contributed more than $300,000 to the campaigns of Texas Supreme Court judges (everyone agreed that had nothing to do with the court's $10.5-*billion* verdict for Pennzoil over Texaco). Everywhere, special interest groups—like the Roofers—look for ways to cover their courtroom bets.

Bad Lawyers, also, generally know where to find cash.

That all sounds a little raw, so we should point out that there is an ethical rule that says a candidate for judge "should not *himself* solicit or accept campaign funds [what?] . . . but he may establish committees of responsible persons to secure and manage the expenditure of funds for his campaign."

Phew!

For a second there, it looked like a candidate would simply have to hope that the Tooth Fairy came around, or something, but it turns out he can set up a committee, which means that lawyers will take care of the money part for him.

There's another hurdle on the political road to becoming a judge, an ethical rule that has exactly the *opposite* of its intended effect. The rule says that a candidate for judge "should *not* make pledges or promises of conduct in office other than the faithful and impartial performance of the duties of the office [*or*] *announce his views on disputed legal or political issues*."

Obviously, the idea was to insulate judicial candidates from the political hurly-burly. But how can that work, when they're running for *election*, trying to get *votes*? If disputed legal and political issues are out-of-bounds, what are judges supposed to talk about on the old campaign trail, the latest fashion in black robes?

The result is that even the most qualified candidates, with the highest integrity, are forced to try to sneak around the rule in laughable ways ("Pssst . . . want to hear my views on abortion?"). Worse, since the rule makes it next to impossible to win by defining a position on issues, judicial candidates are forced back into the arms of political bosses—who can deliver votes without regard to issues.

Indeed, as I learned shortly after receiving Republican party endorsement to run for a long-shot seat in the state legislature, judges seeking political support do not necessarily limit their attentions to the party bosses. In states that choose judges by election, judges may be tempted to do whatever they can for any political figure who wanders into their courtroom.

Or even for a long-shot political hopeful.

I had gone over to City Hall with a routine motion, and expected to wait the normal couple of hours while the judge went through his list. But as soon as I entered the courtroom, His Honor (whom I had met once briefly, at a political reception) spotted me, and immediately interrupted the proceedings.

"I see Mr. Marston is in the courtroom," he announced, to my surprise and embarrassment, "and I'd like to hear his motion."

Guess what?

He granted it.

Since that sort of professional courtesy looks unseemly, or at least injudicious, some states attempt to avoid political pandering by appointing judges, usually on the recommendation of a so-called blue-ribbon panel. That eliminates the need for political contributions, removing most of the cash from the process, but otherwise, the appointment of judges works about the same. It still comes down to knowing the right people, the big difference being that a judicial hopeful needs to know law school deans, business and bar association leaders, distinguished clergy, and so on—instead of politicians.

It's still political.

"Blue-ribbon" really means that the selection is made by members of various elites, accountable to no one, instead of by the citizens at large (even political bosses, after all, are ultimately accountable to voters).

Even nominees to the lofty United States Supreme Court, appointed by the President and subject to Senate confirmation, have to deal with politics.

Ask Robert Bork.

An honors graduate and law review editor at the University of Chicago Law School, professor at Yale Law School, partner at the respected firm of Kirkland and Ellis, former solicitor general of the United States, unanimously confirmed by the U.S. Senate to be judge of the D.C. Circuit, rated by the ABA to be "exceptionally well qualified" for the U.S. Supreme Court, Bork's credentials seemed made-to-order for the high court.

Except for politics.

After a bruising political battle, the Senate voted not to confirm Bork's nomination to the Supreme Court.

Back on the local level, what's the answer?

Appoint judges, or elect them?

Probably some combination of the two systems, with the gag rule that prevents judicial candidates from talking about issues being tossed out. The comprehensive solution for judicial selection, however, is well beyond the scope of this account.

All we're trying to do, having surveyed what Bad Lawyers are up to in the legal profession, is to take a quick snapshot of recent judicial conduct around the country, to see if it's contagious.

Steve Traitz should have met Walter M. Ketchum.

A Chicago lawyer, Ketchum had a situation similar to the one facing Traitz, only in reverse. Ketchum also wanted to give money to a judge, but it was not actually his bright idea. Instead, it was because the judge—Ketchum's old friend Judge Richard LeFevour (in whose courtroom Ketchum conducted about 50 percent of his practice)—kept asking for it. But since they've been doing this for a while in Chicago, Ketchum knew a lawyer cannot just sneak around and slip cash to a judge, even when he asks.

But a lawyer can make a loan to a judge. Or, as it turned out, four or five loans, totaling $5,300.

And when LeFevour had a problem with the insurance company and needed to pay the hospital $10,000 so that his mother could come home for the Christmas holidays, he naturally asked Ketchum. Even for the judge's mom, that seemed a little steep to the attorney, but he wrote to six of his colleagues in practice, and asked them each for $1,000. One refused outright, one was willing until his wife objected (which turned into a world-class "I told you so" once things fell apart), but the other four came up with a grand apiece.

More loans followed.

Except that no one ever got around to details such as interest rates or repayment terms or promissory notes (though the transactions did, for sure, create *invisible* IOUs, which can be the best kind). And, of course, none of the "loans" ever got repaid.

Probably the way it would have worked, had it not been for Operation Greylord, would have been for the loans to be quietly forgiven sometime in the future, maybe when the judge passed away.

But the undercover FBI probe of the Cook County court system—which featured a cooperating judge wearing a microphone in his cowboy boots—exposed the whole scheme. Judge LeFevour was charged with mail fraud, tax fraud, and racketeering—and convicted. Attorney Ketchum got two years in the penalty box.

Fred Lane was another Chicago lawyer—and former Illinois Bar Association president—whose $2,500 "loan" to a Chicago judge was disclosed by Operation Greylord, resulting in his one-year suspension from practice.

"I can't believe this is happening," Lane protested in the *ABA Journal,* "out of this very ethical and moral campaign contribution."

How often do judges take cash?

Looking at the Roofer payoffs in Philadelphia, an easier question would be, how often do they turn it down?

Fifteen judges took it, one turned it down.

But the only way to discover, for certain, the full extent of judicial corruption—since neither the givers nor takers are going to talk about it—is by a massive undercover investigation of an entire court system. Operation Greylord has been the only one of those to date. In eight years, this corruption probe racked up convictions of fifteen judges, forty-five lawyers, eight police officers, ten deputy sheriffs, and three court clerks.

But maybe, as former Chicago U.S. attorney Thomas

P. Sullivan suggested, that was a special situation. "There seems to be in Chicago a pervasive, deep-seated lack of honesty at all levels of government and business," Sullivan charged.

What are bad judges up to everywhere else? It's a familiar list, since bad judges are exposed to the same temptations as Bad Lawyers. Extortion, drugs, and sex are the national favorites, but tax evasion, perjury, and miscellaneous abuses of power are also right up there. Indeed, judges confront all of the temptations faced by lawyers, every day, only *a fortiori,* which is legalese for much stronger.

That's because judges are essentially omnipotent in the courthouse, and generally highly potent outside of it as well, carrying clout with everyone from head waiters to traffic cops. The power that lawyers have in relation to their clients—which, as we've seen, may lead to abuse—is puny compared to the authority that judges can exert over everyone they encounter, on and off the bench.

For example, if a judge, such as His Honor Joseph F. O'Kicki of Cambria County, Pennsylvania, feels like ordering his secretary, as she later testified at his corruption trial, to take dictation while "he had nothing on but a pair of bikini briefs, and he had an erection"—who can stop him?

That's not the sort of thing that gets reversed by the court of appeals.

But the real temptation for judges is money. And unlike lawyers, it's *not* necessarily because they're greedy. The overwhelming majority of judges aspire to the bench because they believe in the system of justice and want to make a contribution. They're willing to accept a tortuous selection process, exhaust personal savings, endure public abuse, work in buildings with lousy air conditioning, and take their chances that the bad guys they put in jail will not come back and kill them.

But, judges still have to buy groceries, fix broken cars and leaky roofs, pay credit card bills and tuitions. And sometimes, looking down from the bench and realizing that the drug dealer standing there handles more loose cash in a week than the judge will see in a career—or, that the Big-Firm lawyer two years out of law school sitting at counsel table earns more, not just than the judge, but more than the Chief Justice of the United States Supreme Court, for heaven's sake—well, there are several ways a judge might react to that.

- He might respond with good-natured ingenuity, as Georgia federal judge Anthony A. Alaimo did, by reducing a lawyer's $100-per-hour fee request to the amount judges make per hour (plus lawyer overhead): $67.50.
- Or, as the Philadelphia judges did, he could simply decide to keep the cash that someone handed him, no one needs to know, maybe use it for Christmas gifts, what's wrong with that (and where did that dull pain come from)?
- A judge could look into other business opportunities, as former Queens, New York, administrative judge Francis X. Smith apparently did, drawing a one-year jail term for lying about his role in the award of a lucrative cable television franchise.
- Or, like Michigan judge Evan Callanan, he might fix a case. Callanan was convicted of conspiring with his lawyer-son to fix the case of a gas station operator charged with sexually molesting a retarded fourteen-year-old girl. FBI agents secretly videotaped the judge taking the payoff in the defendant's car (and also recorded his joking question, "Where are the cameras?"). When sentencing time came, Judge Callanan gave the sex offender three years' probation.

  After conviction on bribery charges, Judge Callanan was sentenced to ten years in federal prison.

Other judges are tripped up by tricks that look more like high jinks than high crimes. A Minnesota Supreme

Court justice took the bar exam just for practice (thinking he might seek admission in another state upon retirement)—and cheated. An Illinois judge was turned in for improperly keeping the fee paid for performing a marriage.

The California Commission on Judicial Qualifications ruled that a judge violated ethical canons when he expressed disbelief in a defendant's testimony "by creating a sound commonly referred to as 'raspberry,' " and gave another defendant "the finger" for coming to court late.

And at traffic courts and justice of the peace chambers everywhere, especially in places with high-powered political machines, some judges look for hand signals flashed up to the bench from committeemen in the audience as they set bail and dispose of cases, just like a hitter taking signs from a third base coach.

Fortunately, the federal court system is different. Appointed by the President for life terms and subject to removal only by impeachment, federal judges are free from the pressures of partisan politics, independent from influence peddlers. Indeed, Roofer boss Steve Traitz, who generally knew his judges, complained, "They get on the [federal] bench, and the only people that can say anythin' to them is God."

Well, not precisely.

The person who talked to U.S. District Judge Alcee L. Hastings of Florida over dinner at the Fontainebleau Hotel did not appear to be a deity; he looked more like a Mafia fixer named Frank Romano. But he was actually an undercover FBI agent, and what he was plotting with the judge was a bribery scheme. A jury acquitted Hastings of conspiring to take a $150,000 bribe, but the evidence was strong enough to persuade the Senate to remove Hastings from the bench by impeachment.

And the man who talked to Mississippi U.S. District Chief Judge Walter L. Nixon, Jr., was just good old Wiley Fairchild, who had steered the judge into some lucrative investments and loaned him the cash to make them. Investigators somehow had the notion that his boy might be involved in smuggling a ton of marijuana into the country, Wiley told Nixon—maybe the judge could put in a good word. No problem, the judge could mention it to his hunting buddy, who happened to be the district attorney.

That might have been innocent, or at least ambiguous, until the judge told the grand jury, under oath, that he had not discussed the Fairchild case with the DA. He was convicted of perjury and sentenced to five years in prison, the first federal judge in American history to be convicted of a crime committed while on the bench.

Doris Adams had a complaint about the way Texas judge Granger McIlhany handled a criminal case involving her two sons, so she wrote him a letter and said so.

That turned out to be a mistake.

The judge ordered her to report to his court and apologize, and after she did, he tossed her into the pokey for twenty-eight days anyway.

In Seattle, investigators compiled an extensive complaint about Judge Gary M. Little, charging that he had improper *ex parte* contacts with numerous young male offenders who were before him for sentencing, entertaining some at his home, others at his vacation cottage. The district attorney's office filed its findings with the Washington Judicial Conduct Commission, the agency charged with acting on complaints against judges.

For seven years, nothing happened, and Judge Little remained on the bench. Then, hours before the *Seattle Post-Intelligencer* published a major exposé charging that Little had sexually exploited teenage boys beginning when he was a teacher at an exclusive Seattle school two decades earlier, he shot himself to death.

In a nutshell, those two cases show why judicial misconduct often goes unpunished.

If you complain to the judge, he might put you in jail.

Or sock you with a fine, as an Alabama judge did when a woman wrote a letter to the editor of a local newspaper, criticizing his handling of her divorce case. Or, if you're a lawyer, His Honor may try to get you disbarred, as Pennsylvania Supreme Court Justice Rolf R. Larsen did when an attorney on the state judicial disciplinary board made public criticisms of Larsen's conduct.

In short, complaints against judges can boomerang unpredictably. Lay criticism can be transformed into contempt of court with a stroke of the gavel, and lawyer critics of judges may see their courtroom success rate plummet—or even face disciplinary charges themselves.

On the other hand, complaints to the state agency in charge of judging judges (called judicial conduct organizations, or JCOs, in the trade) often result in the same official response as the 107-page complaint against Judge Little: Nothing happens.

Déjà vu, we've been here before, no need to dwell on bad judges, except for a couple of observations.

First, the staffing levels of JCOs make the lawyer disciplinary boards look fat. Typically directed by an unpaid board of judges, lawyers, and token lay members, judicial conduct organizations meet monthly or less, and in nearly half the states, the *total* staff consists of a part-time executive director, and a secretary. Only a handful of the fifty judicial disciplinary agencies even employ a full-time investigator.

But second, even though the judgers of judges are more than a little shorthanded, there are sound reasons for protecting judges from frivolous complaints and criticism. Since the time of King Solomon, at least 50 percent of all litigants have been dissatisfied with the results of every judicial proceeding (sometimes, as we've seen, even the winners complain), so judges need insulation from the criticism—and pressures—inherent in the process of trying to dispense justice.

Judges, in short, are *not supposed to be* accountable

in the same way that other public officials are; they are supposed to be independent. That means that the primary responsibility for monitoring judicial conduct should not be in some state agency, or even a JCO. The only people who can really ensure integrity in courtrooms are the two professional groups that work there every day: lawyers and judges.

Jerold Solovy, chairman of the special commission set up in Chicago in response to the corruption revealed by Operation Greylord, put it bluntly. "You cannot have corrupt judges without corrupt lawyers," Solovy stated. "It is my belief that lawyers corrupt judges; judges do not corrupt lawyers. The system is what the lawyers make it."

In Philadelphia, lawyers like Barry Denker made it a system where they could "get the rhythm going with a nickel."

Other lawyers—honest lawyers—said nothing.

In Chicago, forty-five lawyers were eventually convicted of corruption in the court system—but not one lawyer squealed.

The U.S. attorney charged, "There was a guarantee of silence."

But in the Roofer scandal, in which fifteen judges accepted cash in plain envelopes, one judge did speak out strongly, using terms such as "reprehensible" and "breach of trust" to characterize judicial conduct.

The only problem was that the conduct Judge Lisa A. Richette was criticizing was not that of her colleagues who took cash, but rather that of Judge Mary Rose Cunningham, who agreed to cooperate with FBI agents and secretly recorded conversations with other judges.

In the end, though, the Roofers Union cash sent two Philadelphia judges to prison, and resulted in the removal or resignation from the bench of thirteen others. But the careful consideration of these cases by the Supreme Court of Pennsylvania highlights the dangers in making snap judgments.

For example, Judge John J. Chiovero, originally accused of accepting free roofing work from the union, was eventually reinstated by the Pennsylvania high court, even though he had invoked his Fifth Amendment privilege on the financial disclosure form where he should have reported that gift.

Judge Chiovero later amended his financial report, after he remembered that his mother-in-law had actually paid for the new roof.

It took the judge more than three years to remember that, and by the time it popped back into his head, his mother-in-law had unfortunately passed away.

The other Roofer judges are now trying to fight their way back into the Club, to rejoin the ranks of lawyers in good standing. Why not? After all, whatever misdeeds they might have committed were done as judges, not as lawyers.

Or, as former Pennsylvania lawyer disciplinary board chairman James F. Mundy told the *Philadelphia Inquirer:*

"No matter how unethical or villainous a former jurist had shown himself or herself to be while in office, we would be required to welcome that individual's return to the practice of law."

Even, apparantly, if he had malice aforethought.

Eight Quick Tricks To Fix It

(Or, Why the Ozone Layer Will Disappear Before Bad Lawyers Do)

The main obstacle to fixing our profession is that most of us don't want to admit it's broken.

It's not that we're unaware of the outrageous conduct of some lawyers reported day after day. Robert C. Rowe, for example, served four years in the Pennsylvania legislature, ran twice for common pleas court judge—and then made headlines in 1990 when he pleaded guilty to theft, forgery, writing bad checks, and misapplication of entrusted property, adding up to nearly $400,000 of stolen client money.

We shake our heads—a bad apple.

In Philadelphia, we had all seen our colleague Adam O. Renfroe, either around City Hall, or on national TV describing his sensational exposé of drug use in major league baseball. Then we saw him again on TV, this time charged with setting up a $20,000 bribe of a drug case witness; we later learned he had mishandled his clients' bail money, and finally that he had a drug problem of his own.

Another bad apple. Not too surprising, actually, judging from the flashy way he operated; but still, too bad for the profession.

We *were* surprised when popular suburban lawyer David C. Becker disappeared in early 1990, along with $175,000 of his partners' and clients' money. Lawyers who knew him in practice were absolutely certain he was not dishonest. That view became somewhat tenuous, however, when it was disclosed that honest Dave had borrowed $50,000 from a client, putting up his house as security—but neglecting to mention that it was a *rented* house.

(A federal grand jury subsequently indicted Becker on charges of defrauding nine former clients out of $236,505 in personal injury insurance settlements. At this writing, he's still on the lam.)

So we can't shut our eyes to lawyer misconduct, attorneys everywhere see it every day, but we have come up with a couple of ingenious ways to avoid doing anything about it.

If it's just an individual lawyer here and there, we shrug that off, bad apples. Sure, you can quibble about whether it's more than a few, but what's the point? We may have law degrees, but we're still only human, after all. And even though a recent poll *of lawyers* showed that what the respondents do *not* like about their lawyer colleagues is "obnoxiousness," "conceit," and "greed," 80 percent of those polled also said they would become lawyers again if they had the chance. So despite a few mavericks running off to play cowboy or draw comic strips, most of us are not all that dissatisfied with the legal profession.

And when critics attack our profession, if it looks like ignoring the criticism will not work, we use a different approach. Sometimes, we'll decide that the best defense is a tough offense. Even indisputable evidence of widespread lawyer misconduct can be instantly dismissed with a two-word answer: lawyer-bashing.

As noted earlier, having had a couple dozen centuries

to practice ignoring criticism, we're pretty good at it by now. And over the years, we've discovered tactics to turn some of that sniping around, and actually make it work *for* us.

Lawyer-bashing is the current favorite.

That may sound like a casual phrase, but like most things lawyers do casually, it's not. In fact, it's a cleverly designed stratagem that lets us simultaneously ignore criticism and claim sympathy for having been subjected to it. After all, people who have been bashed are not required to explain themselves, and wouldn't any reasonable person be sympathetic to anyone, even a lawyer, who is an innocent bashee?

Once in a long while, though, the legal profession actually responds to public criticism. You might guess that that happens on those rare occasions when we decide a criticism is valid, or during those isolated situations, like Watergate, where the professional abuses are so obvious that it's simply not possible to ignore them.

Well, guess again. It's not valid criticism or widespread lawyer misconduct that snaps the profession into action; it's any threat to the bottom line.

Sure, when general public grumbling about attorneys gets noisy enough to bother us, we'll issue a press release or create another bar association committee. If that doesn't quiet things down, the committee might even hold a hearing or two and issue a report. But that's all a protective smokescreen, purely defensive, not to be confused with actually changing the way we do business. The only time we consider doing that, adopting any serious professional reform, is when we are forced to, or when it looks like there might be money at stake.

We scrubbed the popular Secret Rule setting minimum fees (which *required* a lawyer to collect *at least* the specified fee on every residential property sale, for example, whether he did anything or not), but not because it was widely criticized. We did it because the United States Supreme Court ruled in 1975 that the Virginia bar association's discipline of an enterprising lawyer who charged less than the minimum violated the antitrust laws.

That got our attention.

Even lawyers who have not kept up with legal developments understand that "antitrust" is a ticking time bomb, one that could blow up the entire unregulated legal monopoly. Once the Supreme Court focused the profession's attention on antitrust, lawyers quickly lost interest in minimum fees, scrambling to save those fat *maximum* fees that flow from the monopoly.

Likewise, the longtime ban on lawyer advertising, also the subject of perennial criticism, vanished one day.

Why?

Did lawyers across America all suddenly wake up one morning and decide, Hey, the critics are right, competition is good, we should all put our faces and prices in the yellow pages so clients can decide if they would really rather use the lawyer across the street instead of me?

Not exactly.

Actually, only two lawyers woke up, John R. Bates and Van O. Steen in Arizona, and decided to run a small newspaper ad describing the "legal services at very reasonable rates" offered by their legal clinic. Ever vigilant, the watchdogs of the Arizona bar roared into action, slapping Bates and Steen with a disciplinary proceeding. But the U.S. Supreme Court, again, reversed the pooh-bahs of the bar, ruling in 1977 that the First Amendment protects truthful advertising of legal services.

There are many other examples. But what they all have in common is that unless someone has us up against the wall, grabbing our wallets, lawyers can usually find a noble excuse to avoid doing what's right. But we explain that by arguing that legal issues are much more complicated than laypersons realize.

* * *

- Any reform of the legal profession might undermine the vitality of our adversary system, that unique protector of human liberty.
- The historic independence of the American legal profession and/or judiciary would be threatened by any systematic program to make lawyers and judges behave.
- Even *talking* about lawyer misconduct might make clients afraid to confide in their attorneys, and generally reduce public confidence in the administration of justice.

Reform, then, is risky business.

Once that is understood, even our critics would probably agree that it would be foolish for lawyers to rush in and try any quick fix on the American legal profession. At a minimum, the long-term consequences of any proposed reform would need to be thoroughly studied for a few years by the appropriate ABA committees (and those committees, remember, are likely to be very busy), and lawyers must of course have the opportunity to debate fully the specific language of any changes, which would require a few more years.

Add it all up.

Nothing basic about the Club is going to change any time soon, even if lawyers think it should—and most don't.

But let's play make-believe.

Instead of being cautious lawyers who ponder decisions for decades, let's pretend we're all ferocious NFL linebackers. We don't get paid by the hour, we're not all geniuses, and we never get a fee for explaining why things *can't* be done. But we make megabucks for being expert at our basic task, which is to make snap decisions about which way to move, then do it, like lightning.

Thinking like a linebacker instead of a lawyer, then, assuming that we *had* spotted a few weaknesses in the legal profession over the course of our practice, is there any bold move we could make to clean it up fast?

Could Lawrence Taylor sack the quarterback?

Of course—and the surprising part is it would be pretty simple.

The license to practice is still a privilege, not a right, and the profession has the power to impose conditions on the grant of that privilege. It's the same power that lets us make Secret Rules; all we need are a few new ones, that aren't secret.

Step 1. Squeeze out the cash.

All-time Bad Lawyer Mike Guinan, who was suspected of killing his mistress, certainly cheated on taxes and briefly escaped from prison, started out, according to the *National Law Journal*, stashing cash from his drug clients in forty-two separate bank accounts. Maybe he would have done all of his crimes anyway—but maybe not.

Embezzlement, fraud, drug use, bribery, and tax evasion, to pick an obvious few, are crimes commonly committed by lawyers that are directly linked to the ready cash in the legal profession. Take the cash out of the system, and the opportunity to commit those crimes is dramatically reduced.

After all, what other occupation has billions of dollars in cash sloshing around, with no record-generating cash registers between the payor and payee?

Why not simply ban all cash fees in excess of, say, $500?

What principle of Anglo-Saxon jurisprudence would that undermine?

Of course, even squeezing out the cash fees will not completely dry up cash from the legal system, as former ABA president L. Stanley Chauvin, Jr., recently demonstrated. During the 1990 ABA blowout in Chicago, outgoing President Chauvin was embarrassed to report to the police that some $100 bills had been stolen from his hotel lockbox.

How many?

Well, 550 of them.

That's $55,000 in cash.

But it was *not* a legal fee—and the ABA president assured everyone that it was all legitimate. Chauvin explained that he had simply been asked to hold the cash in escrow pending the outcome of a legitimate dispute between two parties. All part of a busy lawyer's day's work. So our proposed rule would not interfere with legitimate transactions like that (although, just out of curiosity, it would be interesting to know why Chauvin did not counsel his client to go with a nonnegotiable certified check, which fits right into a business envelope, instead of lugging around a suitcaseful of highly stealable C-notes).

Whatever his reason, given Chauvin's leadership of the world's largest lawyer organization, it would obviously be legitimate.

Step 2. Translate the Secret Rules into English that any ten-year-old could understand—and let clients know about the Client Security Fund.

Lawyers shouldn't lie, steal, or cheat.

If they do, they shouldn't be lawyers.

Why can't the Rules just say that?

How would that weaken our adversary system?

(It wouldn't. But to get some idea of how many lawyer loopholes this would eliminate—and of how loud the lawyers would howl if anyone tried this—flip to the back and compare the very different approach of our current Rules.)

And why can't lawyers be required to give a copy of the Rules to each new client, with special mention of the Client Security Fund, where they can go to get their money back if a Bad Lawyer steals it.

Better, why don't we say that lawyers have to put a sticker right there on the door, notifying clients of the Client Fund, just like banks do with the FDIC?

* * *

Step 3. Make all lawyers go to court—and double the pay for judges.

When the aide to Philadelphia judge Kenneth S. Harris told defense lawyer Barry Denker he could "get the rhythm going with a nickel," Denker understood instantly what he meant: It would cost $500 to fix a case.

But where did he learn that?

Certainly not in law school.

He learned it by spending time around the criminal court system. If a larger cross-section of our profession spent time there, two things would happen: Desk-bound practitioners might see what goes on in court and take more interest in the quality of judges and justice as a result; and maybe, just by introducing some new players, we might even clean up that game.

You can test this idea in another way. Compare two worlds by trying this experiment: Stop by the largest law firm in your city, hang out in the reception area for a few minutes, then visit your local courthouse. In most big cities, you'll find exotic flowers, expensive art and lush oriental carpets at your first stop, and urine-stinking corridors, busted air conditioners and down-and-out political fixers at the second.

Then ask yourself this question: If every lawyer who lives in the first world was *required* to spend part of his professional life in the second, do you think conditions in the courthouse, from the filthy corridors to the quality of justice, might be improved?

Part of the problem in our courts, of course, involves what we pay judges. Despite their black robes, there's no reason to think that judges operate much differently than other humans, and we're going to get what we pay for in our courthouses (indeed, given some pay scales around the country, we're probably getting *more* than we're paying for at present).

A couple of decades ago, many of the best practicing lawyers aspired to be judges, the culmination of a career in the law. They still do—but today, many simply cannot afford it. (No one planned on that professional culmination coinciding with the kids' college tuition bills.) Wall Street may have knocked legal pay out of whack, but the men and women who serve as judges are long overdue for a catch-up.

In short, doubling judicial pay would, in a single stroke, make clear that we're willing to spend the money it costs to have a quality justice system.

Step 4. Open up—beef up—and speed up—lawyer discipline.

All attorney discipline should be made public, *at all stages*. That will terrify lots of lawyers at first, and there will be noisy harrumphing around about all those baseless client complaints being aired in public, irresponsible besmirching of our reputations, terrible for public confidence in the system, blah, blah.

But do you know what?

After the initial novelty wears off, it will be *boring*. No one will come, the hearings will not even make the newspapers—except when there's a really Bad Lawyer on the carpet.

The lawyer disciplinary agencies should have enough professional staff so that client complaints can be processed on an expedited timetable. The complaining party should be told, in writing, the disposition of his complaint—and that should happen by a specified deadline, just like requests for government documents under the Freedom of Information Act.

If those federal bureaucrats can do it, why can't we?

Step 5. Require every lawyer to do pro bono *work.*

If you skim the Secret Rules quickly, you might think

that is already required. Rule 6.1, titled "Pro Bono Publico Service," states: "A lawyer should render public interest legal service."

That sounds pretty straightforward. But even with all of the practice so far, we've tricked you again. As used in Rule 6.1, "should" is a Weasel Word, one of the sneakiest in the entire Secret Rules. Because out of more than fifty rules, this provision that *appears* to require lawyers to do public interest work is the *only* rule that does not use the mandatory word "shall" at all.

And just in case someone misses these subtleties and tries to order a lawyer to take a public interest case for no fee, the Comment to Rule 6.1 says that it is "not intended to be enforced through disciplinary process." (How else, one wonders, might a rule get enforced?)

But the behavior of lawyers and the performance of the profession would be improved if lawyers *were* required to contribute some set number of hours to no-pay, public service, cases. Since we're in charge of the machinery of justice, we have an obligation to make justice available to everyone, and anyway, doing an occasional good work would seem like a small price for membership in the lucrative legal monopoly.

And for those lawyers dead set against doing it, maybe we should multiply the required number of *pro bono* hours by their hourly billing rates, and give them the option of contributing that amount to the Little Sisters of the Poor.

If that catches on in New York, home of the $400-an-hour rates, the Little Sisters might have to change their name.

Step 6. Make lawyer discipline the same everywhere—and disbar every lawyer who is convicted of a felony.

The American Bar Association publishes a survey of the lawyer disciplinary systems in each state. The survey is a series of questions (Is the disciplinary agency a permanent one? Do the hearing committees include public members? etc.), and the possible answers are Yes, No, and Other.

There are a total of 107 questions, which offers some idea of the complexity of the crazy-quilt maze we call legal discipline. With these almost endless possibilities for tricks and stunts, as we've seen, Bad Lawyers can often find some loophole to hide out in until the heat's off, if not in their state, then in the one next door.

We should make lawyer discipline simple and make it uniform. An easy first step would be to punch it *all* into a national computer, not just public discipline, but private discipline, malpractice verdicts, client complaints, the whole thing—just like the doctors do.

And if we want a uniform system, we should eliminate the idea of Moral Turpitude (which is really used solely to justify *non*uniform results, exceptions to the rule), and prohibit character witness testimony in lawyer discipline cases—so that members of the Club can no longer rally round to save a popular scoundrel. (After all, if a lawyer-felon has an excellent reputation in the community, who cares? And why should it matter?)

Step 7. Do random audits of lawyer trust accounts.

This is not even a new idea.

New Jersey pioneered the notion of checking, without warning, the accounts where lawyers keep client money. It has been, as you might imagine, somewhat controversial. Even some law-and-order conservatives, like New Jersey Judiciary Committee chairman, Walter M. D. Kern, Jr., were concerned about the audits' potential for privacy invasion and erosion of the attorney-client privilege. In the end, Kern, despite his pro-police background, came out strongly against random audits, calling them "secret police" tactics.

Of course, he made that statement about the time his

disbarment was announced, after the random audit of Kern's own escrow account came up $87,000 short. (He had, as Professor Casner predicted years before, "borrowed" from client money to invest in his own business deals.)

Random audits work, and all lawyers should be subject to them. And despite the howls from attorneys, for most of the twentieth century, similar audits have been a standard accounting practice in every other business.

Step 8. Require law schools to teach students that lawyers should obey the law.

Law professors, as we've seen, might find this to be a controversial concept, but they should ask themselves: Who gets hurt if this crazy idea catches on?

Those eight steps are the openings a linebacker would see, the fast moves we could make to clean up the legal profession.

Probably these proposals will provoke howls from the profession, although we haven't even gotten into the really sensitive areas (the ones where *real money* is involved). We *could* have, for example, talked about breaking up the lawyer monopoly, moving the discipline of the profession to some independent nonlawyer body, and putting limits on runaway fees. These issues should also all be addressed, but they *should* have the sort of deliberate consideration that lawyers like so much.

The eight steps could be implemented immediately.

Wait a second.

We were only playing make-believe.

Which is why the ozone layer is likely to disappear before Bad Lawyers do.

Acknowledgments

Any time you encounter malice aforethought it's a good idea to look for co-conspirators, and there are numerous fingerprints other than mine on the preceding pages.

- Lisa Drew, senior editor at William Morrow and Company, Inc., shaped this book by her insistence that I get off my soapbox and describe how things really work in the legal profession. I am grateful for her perceptive guidance, excellent advice, and consistent enthusiasm.
- Gerry McCauley, an outstanding literary agent, has counseled and encouraged me through previous projects, and was an early supporter of this one; his perspective and insight were extremely valuable.
- William R. Dimeling, with whom I started a practice at Montgomery, McCracken, and who eventually moved into banking and business, is an astute critic of the legal profession, both as a client and a lawyer. Bill is the source of many of the anecdotes and observations in this account.

● W. P. O'Neill, Jr., an international trader who deals with lawyers on several continents, as well as the team at his company, International Raw Materials, Ltd., contributed valuable viewpoints, as clients, and were highly supportive throughout this project.

● Cynthia Roberts, an imaginative writer and editor, tracked down much of the material used here, and also made a significant contribution at an important phase of this project.

Many other lawyers, clients, and others contributed to this account in various ways, and I am grateful to all.

Rules of Professional Conduct as Adopted by the Supreme Court of Pennsylvania Reprinted Without Comments or Code Comparisons (effective April 1, 1988)

Preamble: A Lawyer's Responsibilities

A lawyer is a representative of clients, an officer of the legal system and a public citizen having special responsibility for the quality of justice.

As a representative of clients, a lawyer performs various functions. As advisor, a lawyer provides a client with an informed understanding of the client's legal rights and obligations and explains their practical implications. As advocate, a lawyer zealously asserts the client's position under the rules of the adversary system. As negotiator, a lawyer seeks a result advantageous to the client but consistent with requirements of honest dealing with others. As intermediary between clients, a lawyer seeks to reconcile their divergent interests as an advisor and, to a limited extent, as a spokesperson for each client. A lawyer acts as evaluator by examining a client's legal affairs and reporting about them to the client or to others.

In all professional functions a lawyer should be competent, prompt and diligent. A lawyer should maintain communication with a client concerning the representation. A lawyer should keep in confidence information relating to representation of a client except so far as disclosure is required or permitted by the Rules of Professional Conduct or other law.

A lawyer's conduct should conform to the requirements of the law, both in professional service to clients and in the lawyer's business and personal affairs. A lawyer should use the law's procedures only for legitimate purposes and not to harass or intimidate others. A lawyer should demonstrate respect for the legal system and for those who serve it, including judges, other lawyers and public officials. While it is a lawyer's duty, when necessary, to challenge the rectitude of official action, it is also a lawyer's duty to uphold legal process.

As a public citizen, a lawyer should seek improvement of the law, the administration of justice and the quality of service rendered by the legal profession. As a member of a learned profession, a lawyer should cultivate knowledge of the law beyond its use for clients, employ that knowledge in reform of the law and work to strengthen legal education. A lawyer should be mindful of deficiencies in the administration of justice and of the fact that the poor, and sometimes persons who are not poor, cannot afford adequate legal assistance, and should therefore devote professional time and civic influence in their behalf. A lawyer should aid the legal profession in pursuing these objectives and should help the bar regulate itself in the public interest.

Many of a lawyer's professional responsibilities are prescribed in the Rules of Professional Conduct, as well as substantive and procedural law. However, a lawyer is also guided by personal conscience and the approbation of professional peers. A lawyer should strive to attain the highest level of skill, to improve the law and the legal profession and to exemplify the legal profession's ideals of public service.

A lawyer's responsibilities as a representative of clients, an officer of the legal system and a public citizen are usually harmonious. Thus, when an opposing party is well represented, a lawyer can be a zealous advocate on behalf of a client and at the same time assume that justice is being done. So also, a lawyer can be sure that preserving client confidences ordinarily serves the public interest because people are more likely to seek legal advice, and thereby heed their legal obligations, when they know their communications will be private.

In the nature of law practice, however, conflicting responsibilities are encountered. Virtually all difficult ethical problems arise from conflict between a lawyer's responsibilities to clients, to the legal system and to the lawyer's own interest in remaining an upright person while earning a satisfactory living. The Rules of Professional Conduct prescribe terms of resolving such conflicts. Within the framework of these Rules many difficult issues of professional discretion can arise. Such issues must be resolved through the exercise of sensitive professional and moral judgment guided by the basic principles underlying the Rules.

The legal profession is largely self-governing. Although other professions also have been granted powers of self-government, the legal profession is unique in this respect because of the close relationship between the profession and the processes of government and law enforcement. This connection is manifested in the fact that ultimate authority over the legal profession is vested largely in the courts.

To the extent that lawyers meet the obligations of their professional calling, the occasion for government regulation is obviated. Self-regulation also helps maintain the legal profession's independence from government domination. An independent legal profession is an important force in preserving government under law, for abuse of legal authority is more readily challenged by a profession whose members are not dependent on government for the right to practice.

The legal profession's relative autonomy carries with it special responsibilities of self-government. The profession has a responsibility to assure that its regulations are conceived in the public interest and not in furtherance of parochial or self-interested concerns of the bar. Every lawyer is responsible for observance of the Rules of Professional Conduct. A lawyer should also aid in securing their observance by other lawyers. Neglect of these responsibilities compromises the independence of the profession and the public interest which it serves.

Lawyers play a vital role in the preservation of society. The fulfillment of this role requires an understanding by lawyers of their relationship to our legal system. The Rules of Professional Conduct, when properly applied, serve to define that relationship.

SCOPE

The Rules of Professional Conduct are rules of reason. They should be interpreted with reference to the purposes of legal representation and of the law itself. Some of the Rules are imperatives, cast in the terms "shall" or "shall not." These define proper conduct for purposes of professional discipline. Others, generally cast in the term "may" or "should," are permissive and define areas under the Rules in which the lawyer has professional discretion. No disciplinary action should be taken when the lawyer chooses not to act or acts within the bounds of such discretion. Other Rules define the nature of relationships between the lawyer and others. The Rules are thus partly obligatory and disciplinary and partly constitutive and descriptive in that they define a lawyer's professional role. Many of the Comments use the term "should." Comments do not add obligations to the Rules but provide guidance for practicing in compliance with the Rules.

The Rules presuppose a larger legal context shaping the lawyer's role. That context includes court rules and statutes relating to matters of licensure, laws defining specific obligations of lawyers and substantive and procedural law in general. Compliance with the Rules, as with all law in an open society, depends primarily upon understanding and voluntary compliance, secondarily upon reinforcement by peer and public opinion and finally, when necessary, upon enforcement through disciplinary proceedings. The Rules do not, however, exhaust the moral and ethical considerations that should inform a lawyer, for no worthwhile human activity can be completely defined by legal rules.

The Rules simply provide a framework for the ethical practice of law.

Furthermore, for purposes of determining the lawyer's authority and responsibility, principles of substantive law external to these Rules determine whether a client-lawyer relationship exists. Most of the duties flowing from the client-lawyer relationship attach only after the client has requested the lawyer to render legal services and the lawyer has agreed to do so. But there are some duties, such as that of confidentiality under Rule 1.6, that may attach when the lawyer agrees to consider whether a client-lawyer relationship shall be established. Whether a client-lawyer relationship exists for any specific purpose can depend on the circumstances and may be a question of fact.

Under various legal provisions, including constitutional, statutory and common law, the responsibilities of government lawyers may include authority concerning legal matters that ordinarily reposes in the client in private client-lawyer relationships. For example, a lawyer for a government agency may have authority on behalf of the government to decide upon settlement or whether to appeal from an adverse judgment. Such authority in various respects is generally vested in the attorney general and the state's attorney in state government, and their federal counterparts, and the same may be true of other government law officers. Also, lawyers under the supervision of these officers may be authorized to represent several government agencies in intragovernmental legal controversies in circumstances where a private lawyer could not represent multiple private clients. They also may have authority to represent the "public interest" in circumstances where a private lawyer would not be authorized to do so. These Rules do not abrogate any such authority.

Failure to comply with an obligation or prohibition imposed by a Rule is a basis for invoking the disciplinary process. The Rules presuppose that disciplinary assessment of a lawyer's conduct will be made on the basis of the facts and circumstances as they existed at the time of the conduct in question and in recognition of the fact that a lawyer often has to act upon uncertain or incomplete evidence of the situation. Moreover, the Rules presuppose that whether or not discipline should be imposed for a violation, and the severity of a sanction, depend on all the circumstances, such as the willfulness and seriousness of the violation, extenuating factors and whether there have been previous violations.

Violation of a Rule should not give rise to a cause of action nor should it create any presumption that a legal duty has been breached. The Rules are designed to provide guidance to lawyers and to provide a structure for regulating conduct through disciplinary agencies. They are not designed to be a basis for civil liability. Furthermore, the purpose of the Rules can be subverted when they are invoked by opposing parties as procedural weapons. The fact that a Rule is a just basis for a lawyer's self-assessment, or for sanctioning a lawyer under the administration of a disciplinary authority, does not imply that an antagonist in a collateral proceeding or transaction has standing to seek enforcement of the Rule. Accordingly, nothing in the Rules should be deemed to augment any substantive legal duty of lawyers or the extra-disciplinary consequences of violating such a duty.

Moreover, these Rules are not intended to govern or affect judicial application of either the attorney-client or work product privilege. Those privileges were developed to promote compliance with law and fairness in litigation. In reliance on the attorney-client privilege, clients are entitled to expect that communications within the scope of the privilege will be protected against compelled disclosure. The attorney-client privilege is that of the client and not of the lawyer. The fact that in exceptional situations the lawyer under the Rules has a limited discretion to disclose a client confidence does not vitiate the proposition that, as a general matter, the client has a reasonable expectation that information relating to the client will not be voluntarily disclosed and that disclosure of such information may be judicially compelled only in accordance with recognized exceptions to the attorney-client and work product privileges.

The lawyer's exercise of discretion not to disclose information under Rule 1.6 should not be subject to reexamination. Permitting such reexamination would be incompatible with the general policy of promoting compliance with law through assurances that communications will be protected against disclosure. These Rules were derived from the Model Rules of Professional Conduct adopted by the American Bar Association in 1983 as amended. The Rules omit some provisions that appear in the ABA Model Rules of Professional Conduct. The omissions should not be interpreted as condoning behavior proscribed by the omitted provision.

The Comment accompanying each Rule explains and illustrates the meaning and purpose of the Rule. The Preamble and this note on Scope provide general orientation. The Comments are intended as guides to interpretation, but the text of each Rule is authoritative. Code Comparisons were prepared to compare counterparts in the Code of Professional Responsibility. The notes have not been adopted, do not constitute part of the Rules, and are not intended to affect the application or interpretation of the Rules and Comments.

TERMINOLOGY

"Belief" or "Believes" denotes that the person involved actually supposed the fact in question to be true. A person's belief may be inferred from circumstances.

"Consult" or "Consultation" denotes communication of information reasonably sufficient to permit the client to appreciate the significance of the matter in question.

"Firm" or "Law firm" denotes a lawyer or lawyers in a private firm, lawyers employed in the legal department of a corporation or other organization and lawyers employed in a legal services organization. See Comment, Rule 1.10.

"Fraud" or "Fraudulent" denotes conduct having a purpose to deceive and not merely negligent misrepresentation or failure to apprise another of relevant information.

"Knowingly," "Known," or "Knows" denotes actual knowledge of the fact in question. A person's knowledge may be inferred from circumstances.

"Partner" denotes a member of a partnership and a shareholder in a law firm organized as a professional corporation.

"Reasonable" or "Reasonably" when used in relation to conduct by a lawyer denotes the conduct of a reasonably prudent and competent lawyer.

"Reasonable belief" or "Reasonably believes" when used in reference to a lawyer denotes that the lawyer believes the matter in question and that the circumstances are such that the belief is reasonable.

"Reasonably should know" when used in reference to a lawyer denotes that a lawyer of reasonable prudence and competence would ascertain the matter in question.

"Substantial" when used in reference to degree or extent denotes a material matter of clear and weighty importance.

CLIENT-LAWYER RELATIONSHIP

RULE 1.1 Competence

A lawyer shall provide competent representation to a client. Competent representation requires the legal knowledge, skill, thoroughness and preparation necessary for the representation.

RULE 1.2 Scope of Representation

(a) A lawyer shall abide by a client's decisions concerning the objectives of representation, subject to paragraphs (c), (d) and (e), and shall consult with the client as to the means by which they are to be pursued. A lawyer shall abide by a client's decision whether to accept an offer of settlement of a matter. In a criminal case, the lawyer shall abide by the client's decision, after consultation with the lawyer, as to a plea to be entered, whether to waive jury trial and whether the client will testify.

(b) A lawyer's representation of a client, including representation by appointment, does not constitute an endorsement of the client's political, economic, social or moral views or activities.

(c) A lawyer may limit the objectives of the representation if the client consents after consultation.

(d) A lawyer shall not counsel a client to engage, or assist a client, in conduct that the lawyer knows is criminal or fraudulent, but a lawyer may discuss the legal consequences of any proposed course of conduct with a client and may counsel or assist a client to make a good faith effort to determine the validity, scope, meaning or application of the law.

(e) When a lawyer knows that a client expects assistance not permitted by the Rules of Professional Conduct or other law, the lawyer shall consult with the client regarding the relevant limitations on the lawyer's conduct.

RULE 1.3 Diligence

A lawyer shall act with reasonable diligence and promptness in representing a client.

RULE 1.4 Communication

(a) A lawyer shall keep a client informed about the status of a matter and promptly comply with reasonable requests for information.

(b) A lawyer shall explain a matter to the extent reasonably necessary to permit the client to make informed decisions regarding the representation.

RULE 1.5 Fees

(a) A lawyer shall not enter into an agreement for, charge, or collect an illegal or clearly excessive fee. The factors to be considered in determining the propriety of a fee include the following:

(1) whether the fee is fixed or contingent;

(2) the time and labor required, the novelty and difficulty of the questions involved, and the skill requisite to perform the legal service properly;

(3) the likelihood, if apparent to the client, that the acceptance of the particular employment will preclude other employment by the lawyer;

(4) the fee customarily charged in the locality for similar legal services;

(5) the amount involved and the results obtained;

(6) the time limitations imposed by the client or by the circumstances;

(7) the nature and length of the professional relationship with the client; and

(8) the experience, reputation, and ability of the lawyer or lawyers performing the services.

(b) When the lawyer has not regularly represented the client, the basis or rate of the fee shall be communicated to the client, in writing, before or within a reasonable time after commencing the representation.

(c) A fee may be contingent on the outcome of the matter for which the service is rendered, except in a matter in which a contingent fee is prohibited by paragraph (d) or other law. A contingent fee agreement shall be in writing and shall state the method by which the fee is to be determined, including the percentage or percentages that shall accrue to the lawyer in the event of settlement, trial or appeal, litigation and other expenses to be deducted from the recovery, and whether such expenses are to be deducted before or after the contingent fee is calculated. Upon conclusion of a contingent fee matter, the lawyer shall provide the client with a written statement stating the outcome of the matter and, if there is a recovery, showing the remittance to the client and the method of its determination.

(d) A lawyer shall not enter into an arrangement for, charge, or collect:

(1) any fee in a domestic relations matter, the payment or amount of which is contingent upon the securing of a divorce or upon the amount of alimony or support; or

(2) a contingent fee for representing a defendant in a criminal case.

(e) A lawyer shall not divide a fee for legal services with another lawyer who is not in the same firm unless:

(1) the client is advised of and does not object to the participation of all the lawyers involved, and

(2) the total fee of the lawyers is not illegal or clearly excessive for all legal services they rendered the client.

RULE 1.6 Confidentiality of Information

(a) A lawyer shall not reveal information relating to representation of a client unless the client consents after consultation, except for disclosures that are impliedly authorized in order to carry out the representation, and except as stated in paragraph (b) and (c).

(b) A lawyer shall reveal such information if necessary to comply with the duties stated in Rule 3.3.

(c) A lawyer may reveal such information to the extent the lawyer reasonably believes necessary:

(1) to prevent the client from committing a criminal act that the lawyer believes is likely to result in death or substantial bodily harm or substantial injury to the financial interests or property of another;

(2) to prevent or to rectify the consequences of a client's criminal or fraudulent act in the commission of which the lawyer's services are being or had been used; or

(3) to establish a claim or defense on behalf of the lawyer in a controversy between the lawyer and the client, to establish a defense to a criminal charge or civil claim or disciplinary proceeding against the lawyer based upon conduct in which the client was involved, or to respond to allegations in any proceeding concerning the lawyer's representation of the client.

(d) The duty not to reveal information relating to representation of a client continues after the client-lawyer relationship has terminated.

RULE 1.7 Conflict of Interest: General Rule

(a) A lawyer shall not represent a client if the representation of that client will be directly adverse to another client, unless:

(1) the lawyer reasonably believes the representation will not adversely affect the relationship with the other client; and

(2) each client consents after consultation.

(b) A lawyer shall not represent a client if the representation of that client may be materially limited by the lawyer's responsibilities to another client or to a third person, or by the lawyer's own interests, unless:

(1) the lawyer reasonably believes the representation will not be adversely affected; and

(2) the client consents after full disclosure and consultation. When representation of multiple clients in a single matter is undertaken, the consultation shall include explanation of the implications of the common representation and the advantages and risks involved.

RULE 1.8 Conflict of Interest: Prohibited Transactions

(a) A lawyer shall not enter into a business transaction with a client or knowingly acquire an ownership, possessory, security or other pecuniary interest adverse to a client unless:

(1) the transaction and terms on which the lawyer acquires the interest are fully disclosed and transmitted in writing to the client in a manner which can be reasonably understood by the client;

(2) the client is advised and is given a reasonable opportunity to seek the advice of independent counsel in the transaction; and

(3) the client consents in writing thereto.

(b) A lawyer shall not use information relating to representation of a client to the disadvantage of the client unless the client consents after consultation.

(c) A lawyer shall not prepare an instrument giving the lawyer or a person related to the lawyer as parent, child, sibling, or spouse any substantial gift from a client, including a testamentary gift, except where the client is related to the donee within the third degree of relationship.

(d) Prior to the conclusion of representation of a client, a lawyer shall not make or negotiate an agreement giving the lawyer literary or media rights to a portrayal or account based in substantial part on information relating to the representation.

(e) A lawyer shall not provide financial assistance to a client in connection with pending or contemplated litigation, except that:

(1) a lawyer may advance court costs and expenses of litigation, the repayment of which may be contingent on the outcome of the matter; and

(2) a lawyer representing an indigent client may pay court costs and expenses of litigation on behalf of the client.

(f) A lawyer shall not accept compensation for representing a client from one other than the client unless:

(1) the client consents after full disclosure of the circumstances and consultation;

(2) there is no interference with the lawyer's independence of professional judgment or with the client-lawyer relationship; and

(3) information relating to representation of a client is protected as required by Rule 1.6.

(g) A lawyer who represents two or more clients shall not participate in making an aggregate settlement of the claims of or against the clients, or in a criminal case an aggregated agreement as to guilty or nolo contendere pleas, unless each client consents after consultation, including disclosure of the existence and nature of all the claims or pleas involved and of the participation of each person in the settlement.

(h) A lawyer shall not make an agreement prospectively limiting the lawyer's liability to a client for malpractice unless permitted by law and the client is independently represented in making the agreement, nor shall a lawyer settle a claim for such liability with an unrepresented client or former client without first advising that person in writing that independent representation is appropriate in connection therewith.

(i) A lawyer related to another lawyer as parent, child, sibling, or spouse shall not represent a client in a representation directly adverse to a person who the lawyer knows is represented by the other lawyer except upon consent by the client after consultation regarding the relationship.

(j) A lawyer shall not acquire a proprietary interest in a cause of action that the lawyer is conducting for a client, except that the lawyer may:

(1) acquire a lien granted by law to secure the lawyer's fee or expenses; and

(2) contract with a client for a reasonable contingent fee in a civil case.

RULE 1.9 Conflict of Interest: Former Client

A lawyer who has formerly represented a client in a matter shall not thereafter:

(a) represent another person in the same or a substantially related matter in which that person's interests are materially adverse to the interests of the former client unless the former client consents after a full disclosure of the circumstances and consultation; or

(b) use information relating to the representation to the disadvantage of the former client except as Rule 1.6 would permit with respect to a client or when the information has become generally known.

RULE 1.10 Imputed Disqualification: General Rule

(a) While lawyers are associated in a firm, none of them shall knowingly represent a client when any one of them practicing alone would be prohibited from doing so by Rules 1.7, 1.8(c), 1.9 or 2.2.

(b) When a lawyer becomes associated with a firm, the firm may not knowingly represent a person in the same or a substantially related matter in which that lawyer, or a firm with which the lawyer was associated, had previously represented a client whose interests are materially adverse to that person and about whom the lawyer had acquired information protected by Rules 1.6 and 1.9(b) that is material to the matter unless:

(1) the disqualified lawyer is screened from any participation in the matter and is apportioned no part of the fee therefrom; and

(2) written notice is promptly given to the appropriate client to enable it to ascertain compliance with the provisions of this Rule.

(c) When a lawyer has terminated an association with a firm, the firm is not prohibited from thereafter representing a person with interests materially adverse to those of a client represented by the formerly associated lawyer unless:

(1) the matter is the same or substantially related to that in which the formerly associated lawyer represented the client; and

(2) any lawyer remaining in the firm has information protected by Rules 1.6 and 1.9(b) that is material to the matter.

(d) A disqualification prescribed by this Rule may be waived by the affected client under the conditions stated in Rule 1.7.

RULE 1.11 Successive Government and Private Employment

(a) Except as law may otherwise expressly permit, a lawyer shall not represent a private client in connection with a matter in which the lawyer participated personally and substantially as a public officer or employee, unless the appropriate government agency consents after consultation. No lawyer in a firm with which that lawyer is associated may knowingly undertake or continue representation in such a matter unless:

(1) the disqualified lawyer is screened from any participation in the matter and is apportioned no part of the fee therefrom; and

(2) written notice is promptly given to the appropriate government agency to enable it to ascertain compliance with the provisions of this rule.

(b) Except as law may otherwise expressly permit, a lawyer having information that the lawyer knows is confidential government information about a person acquired when the lawyer was a public officer or employee, may not represent a private client whose interests are adverse to that person in a matter in which the information could be used to the material disadvantage of that person. A firm with which that lawyer is associated may undertake or continue representation in the matter only if the disqualified lawyer is screened from any participation in the matter and is apportioned no part of the fee therefrom.

(c) Except as law may otherwise expressly permit, a lawyer serving as a public officer or employee shall not:

(1) participate in a matter in which the lawyer participated personally and substantially while in private practice or non-governmental employment, unless under applicable law no one is, or by lawful delegation may be, authorized to act in the lawyer's stead in the matter; or

(2) negotiate for private employment with any person who is involved as a party or as attorney for a party in a matter in which the lawyer is participating personally and substantially.

(d) As used in this Rule, the term "matter" includes:

(1) any judicial or other proceeding, application, request for a ruling or other determination, contract, claim, controversy, investigation, charge, accusation, arrest or other particular matter involving a specific party or parties; and

(2) any other matter covered by the conflict of interest rules of the appropriate government agency.

(e) As used in this Rule, the term "confidential government information" means information which has been obtained under governmental authority and which, at the time this Rule is applied, the government is prohibited by law from disclosing to the public or has a legal privilege not to disclose, and which is not otherwise available to the public.

RULE 1.12 Former Judge or Arbitrator or Law Clerk

(a) Except as stated in paragraph (d), a lawyer shall not represent anyone in connection with a matter in which the lawyer participated personally and substantially as a judge or other adjudicative officer, arbitrator or law clerk to such a person, unless all parties to the proceeding consent after disclosure.

(b) A lawyer shall not negotiate for employment with any person who is involved as a party or as attorney for a party in a matter in which the lawyer is participating personally and substantially as a judge or other adjudicative officer, or arbitrator.

A lawyer serving as a law clerk to a judge, other adjudicative officer or arbitrator may negotiate for employment with a party or attorney involved in a matter in which the clerk is participating personally and substantially, but only after the lawyer has notified the judge, other adjudicative officer or arbitrator.

(c) If a lawyer is disqualified by paragraph (a), no lawyer in a firm with which that lawyer is associated may knowingly undertake or continue representation in the matter unless:

(1) the disqualified lawyer is screened from any participation in the matter and is apportioned no part of the fee therefrom; and

(2) written notice is promptly given to the appropriate tribunal to enable it to ascertain compliance with the provisions of this rule.

(d) An arbitrator selected as a partisan of a party in a multimember arbitration panel is not prohibited from subsequently representing that party.

RULE 1.13 Organization as Client

(a) A lawyer employed or retained by an organization represents the organization acting through its duly authorized constituents.

(b) If a lawyer for an organization knows that an officer, employee or other person associated with the organization is engaged in action, intends to act or refuses to act in a matter related to the representation that is a violation of legal obligation to the organization, or a violation of law which reasonably might be imputed to the organization, and is likely to result in substantial injury to the organization, the lawyer shall proceed as is reasonably necessary in the best interest of the organization. In determining how to proceed, the lawyer shall give due consideration to the seriousness of the violation and its consequences, the scope and nature of the lawyer's representation, and responsibility in the organization concerning such matters and any other relevant considerations. Any measures taken shall be designed to minimize disruption of the organization and the risk of revealing information relating to the representation to persons outside the organization. Such measures may include among others:

(1) asking reconsideration of the matter;

(2) advising that a separate legal opinion on the matter be sought for presentation to appropriate authority in the organization; and

(3) referring the matter to higher authority in the organization, including, if warranted by the seriousness of the matter, referral to the highest authority that can act in behalf of the organization as determined by applicable law.

(c) If, despite the lawyer's efforts in accordance with paragraph (b), the highest authority that can act on behalf of the organization insists upon action, or a refusal to act, that is clearly a violation of law and is likely to result in substantial injury to the organization, the lawyer may resign in accordance with Rule 1.16.

(d) In dealing with an organization's directors, officers, employees, members, shareholders or other constituents, a lawyer shall explain the identity of the client when it is apparent that the organization's interests are adverse to those of the constituents with whom the lawyer is dealing.

(e) A lawyer representing an organization may also represent any of its directors, officers, employees, members, shareholders or other constituents, subject to the provisions of Rule 1.7. If the organization's consent to the dual representation is required by Rule 1.7, the consent shall be given by an appropriate official of the organization other than the individual who is to be represented, or by the shareholders.

RULE 1.14 Clients Under a Disability

(a) When a client's ability to make adequately considered decisions in connection with the representation is impaired, whether because of minority, mental disability or for some other reason, the lawyer shall, as far as reasonably possible, maintain a normal client-lawyer relationship with the client.

(b) A lawyer may seek the appointment of a guardian or take other protective action with respect to a client, only when the lawyer reasonably believes that the client cannot adequately act in the client's own interest.

RULE 1.15 Safekeeping Property

(a) A lawyer shall hold property of clients or third persons that is in a lawyer's possession in connection with a representation separate from the lawyer's own property. Funds shall be kept in a separate account maintained in the state where the lawyer's office is situated, or elsewhere with the consent of the client or third person. Other property shall be identified as such and appropriately safeguarded. Complete records of such account funds and other property shall be preserved for a period of five years after termination of the representation.

(b) Upon receiving funds or other property in which a client or third person has an interest, a lawyer shall promptly notify the client or third person. Except as stated in this Rule or otherwise permitted by law or by agreement with the client, a lawyer shall promptly deliver to the client or third person any funds or other property that the client or third person is entitled to receive and, upon request by the client or third person, shall promptly render a full accounting regarding such property.

(c) When in the course of representation a lawyer is in possession of property in which both the lawyer and another person claim interest, the property shall be kept separate by the lawyer until there is an accounting and severance of their interests. If a dispute arises concerning their respective interests, the portion in dispute shall be kept separate by the lawyer until the dispute is resolved.

RULE 1.16 Declining or Terminating Representation

(a) Except as stated in paragraph (c), a lawyer shall not represent a client or, where representation has commenced, shall withdraw from the representation of a client if:

(1) the representation will result in violation of the rules of professional conduct or other law;

(2) the lawyer's physical or mental condition materially impairs the lawyer's ability to represent the client; or

(3) the lawyer is discharged.

(b) Except as stated in paragraph (c), a lawyer may withdraw from representing a client if withdrawal can be accomplished without material adverse effect on the interests of the client, or if:

(1) the client persists in a course of action involving the lawyer's services that the lawyer reasonably believes is criminal or fraudulent;

(2) the client has used the lawyer's services to perpetrate a crime or fraud;

(3) a client insists upon pursuing an objective that the lawyer considers repugnant or imprudent;

(4) the client fails substantially to fulfill an obligation to the lawyer regarding the lawyer's services and has been given reasonable warning that the lawyer will withdraw unless the obligation is fulfilled;

(5) the representation will result in an unreasonable financial burden on the lawyer or has been rendered unreasonably difficult by the client; or

(6) other good cause for withdrawal exists.

(c) When ordered to do so by a tribunal, a lawyer shall continue representation notwithstanding good cause for terminating the representation.

(d) Upon termination of representation, a lawyer shall take steps to the extent reasonably practicable to protect a client's interests, such as giving reasonable notice to the client, allowing time for employment of other counsel, surrendering papers and property to which the client is entitled and refunding any advance payment of fee that has not been earned. The lawyer may retain papers relating to the client to the extent permitted by other law.

COUNSELOR

RULE 2.1 Advisor

In representing a client, a lawyer should exercise independent professional judgment and render candid advice. In rendering advice, a lawyer may refer not only to law but to other considerations such as moral, economic, social and political factors, that may be relevant to the client's situation.

RULE 2.2 Intermediary

(a) A lawyer may act as intermediary between clients if:

(1) the lawyer consults with each client concerning the implications of the common representation, including the advantages and risks involved, and the effect on the attorney-client privileges, and obtains each client's consent to the common representation;

(2) the lawyer reasonably believes that the matter can be resolved on terms compatible with the clients' best interests, that each client will be able to make adequately informed decisions in the matter and that there is little risk of material prejudice to the interest of any of the clients if the contemplated resolution is unsuccessful; and

(3) the lawyer reasonably believes that the common representation can be undertaken impartially and without improper effect on other responsibilities the lawyer has to any of the clients.

(b) While acting as intermediary, the lawyer shall consult with each client concerning the decisions to be made and the considerations relevant in making them, so that each client can make adequately informed decisions.

(c) A lawyer shall withdraw as intermediary if any of the clients so request, or if any of the conditions stated in paragraph (a) is no longer satisfied. Upon withdrawal, the lawyer shall not continue to represent any of the clients in the matter that was the subject of the intermediation.

RULE 2.3 Evaluation for Use by a Third Person

(a) A lawyer may undertake an evaluation of a matter affecting a client for the use of someone other than the client if:

(1) the lawyer reasonably believes that making the evaluation is compatible with other aspects of the lawyer's relationship with the client; and

(2) the client consents after consultation.

(b) Except as disclosure is required in connection with a report of an evaluation, information relating to the evaluation is otherwise protected by Rule 1.6.

ADVOCATE

RULE 3.1 Meritorious Claims and Contentions

A lawyer shall not bring or defend a proceeding, or assert or controvert an issue therein, unless there is a basis for doing so that is not frivolous, which includes a good faith argument for an extension, modification or reversal of existing law. A lawyer for the defendant in a criminal proceeding, or the respondent in a proceeding that could result in incarceration, may nevertheless so defend the proceeding as to require that every element of the case be established.

RULE 3.2 Expediting Litigation

A lawyer shall make reasonable efforts to expedite litigation consistent with the interests of the client.

RULE 3.3 Candor Toward the Tribunal

(a) A lawyer shall not knowingly:

(1) make a false statement of material fact or law to a tribunal;

(2) fail to disclose a material fact to a tribunal when disclosure is necessary to avoid assisting a criminal or fraudulent act by the client;

(3) fail to disclose to the tribunal legal authority in the controlling jurisdiction known to the lawyer to be directly adverse to the position of the client and not disclosed by opposing counsel; or

(4) offer evidence that the lawyer knows to be false. If a lawyer has offered material evidence and comes to know of its falsity, the lawyer shall take reasonable remedial measures.

(b) The duties stated in paragraph (a) continue to the conclusion of the proceeding, and apply even if compliance requires disclosure of information otherwise protected by Rule 1.6.

(c) A lawyer may refuse to offer evidence that the lawyer reasonable believes is false.

(d) In an ex parte proceeding, a lawyer shall inform the tribunal of all material facts known to the lawyer which will enable the tribunal to make an informed decision, whether or not the facts are adverse.

RULE 3.4 Fairness to Opposing Party and Counsel

A lawyer shall not:

(a) unlawfully obstruct another party's access to evidence or unlawfully alter, destroy or conceal a document or other material having potential evidentiary value or assist another person to do any such act;

(b) falsify evidence, counsel or assist a witness to testify falsely, pay, offer to pay, or acquiesce in the payment of compensation to a witness contingent upon the content of the witness' testimony or the outcome of the case; but a lawyer may pay, cause to be paid, guarantee or acquiesce in the payment of:

(1) expenses reasonably incurred by a witness in attending or testifying,

(2) reasonable compensation to a witness for the witness' loss of time in attending or testifying, and

(3) a reasonable fee for the professional services of an expert witness;

(c) When appearing before a tribunal, assert the lawyer's personal opinion as to the justness of a cause, as to the credibility of a witness, as to the culpability of a civil litigant, or as to the guilt or innocence of an accused; but the lawyer may argue, on the lawyer's analysis of the evidence, for any position or conclusion with respect to the matters stated herein; or

(d) request a person other than a client to refrain from voluntarily giving relevant information to another party unless:

(1) the person is a relative or an employee or other agent of a client; and

(2) the lawyer reasonably believes that the person's interests will not be adversely affected by refraining from giving such information and such conduct is not prohibited by Rule 4.2.

RULE 3.5 Impartiality and Decorum of the Tribunal

A lawyer shall not:

(a) seek to influence a judge, juror, prospective juror or other official by means prohibited by law;

(b) communicate ex parte with such a person except as permitted by law; or

(c) engage in conduct disruptive to a tribunal.

RULE 3.6 Trial Publicity

(a) A lawyer shall not make an extrajudicial statement that a reasonable person would expect to be disseminated by means of public communication if the lawyer knows or reasonably should know that it will have a substantial likelihood of materially prejudicing an adjudicative proceeding.

(b) A statement referred to in paragraph (a) ordinarily is likely to have such an effect when it refers to a civil matter triable to a jury, a criminal matter, or any other proceeding that could result in incarceration, and the statement relates to:

(1) the character, credibility, reputation or criminal record of a party, suspect in a criminal investigation or witness, or the identity of a witness, or the expected testimony of a party or witness;

(2) in a criminal case or proceeding that could result in incarceration, the possibility of a plea of guilty to the offense or the existence or contents of any confession, admission, or statement given by a defendant or suspect or that person's refusal or failure to make a statement;

(3) the performance or results of any examination or test or the refusal or failure of a person to submit to an examination or test, or the identity or nature of physical evidence expected to be presented;

(4) any opinion as to the guilt or innocence of a defendant or suspect in a criminal case or proceeding that could result in incarceration;

(5) information the lawyer knows or reasonably should know is likely to be inadmissible as evidence in a trial and would if disclosed create a substantial risk of prejudicing an impartial trial; or

(6) the fact that a defendant has been charged with a crime, unless there is included therein a statement explaining that the charge is merely an accusation and that the defendant is presumed innocent until and unless proven guilty.

(c) Notwithstanding paragraph (a) and (b) (1–5), a lawyer involved in the investigation or litigation of a matter may state without elaboration:

(1) the general nature of the claim or defense;

(2) the information contained in a public record;

(3) that an investigation of the matter is in progress, including the general scope of the investigation, the offense or claim or defense involved and, except when prohibited by law, the identity of the persons involved;

(4) the scheduling or result of any step in litigation;

(5) a request for assistance in obtaining evidence and information necessary thereto;

(6) a warning of danger concerning the behavior of a person involved, when there is reason to believe that there exists the likelihood of substantial harm to an individual or to the public interest; and

(7) in a criminal case:

(i) the identity, residence, occupation and family status of the accused;

(ii) if the accused has not been apprehended, information necessary to aid in apprehension of that person;

(iii) the fact, time and place of arrest; and

(iv) the identity of investigating and arresting officers or agencies and the length of the investigation.

RULE 3.7 Lawyer as Witness

(a) A lawyer shall not act as advocate at a trial in which the lawyer is likely to be a necessary witness except where:

(1) the testimony relates to an uncontested issue;

(2) the testimony relates to the nature and value of legal services rendered in the case; or

(3) disqualification of the lawyer would work substantial hardship on the client.

(b) A lawyer may act as advocate in a trial in which another lawyer in the lawyer's firm is likely to be called as a witness unless precluded from doing so by Rule 1.7 or Rule 1.9.

RULE 3.8 Special Responsibilities of a Prosecutor

The prosecutor in a criminal case shall:

(a) refrain from prosecuting a charge that the prosecutor knows is not supported by probable cause;

(b) make reasonable efforts to assure that the accused has been advised of the right to, and the procedure for obtaining, counsel and has been given reasonable opportunity to obtain counsel;

(c) not seek to obtain from an unrepresented accused a waiver of important pretrial rights, such as the right to a preliminary hearing;

(d) make timely disclosure to the defense of all evidence or information known to the prosecutor that tends to negate the guilt of the accused or mitigates the offense, and, in connection with sentencing, disclose to the defense and to the tribunal all unprivileged mitigating information known to the prosecutor, except when the prosecutor is relieved of this responsibility by a protective order of the tribunal; and

(e) exercise reasonable care to prevent investigators, law enforcement personnel, employees or other persons assisting or associated with the prosecutor in a criminal case from making an extrajudicial statement that the prosecutor would be prohibited from making under Rule 3.6.

RULE 3.9 Advocate in Nonadjudicative Proceedings

A lawyer representing a client before a legislative or administrative tribunal in a nonadjudicative proceeding shall disclose that the appearance is in a representative capacity and shall conform to the provisions of Rules 3.3(a) through (c), 3.4(a) and (b), and 3.5.

RULE 3.10. Issuance of Subpoenas to Lawyers

A public prosecutor or other governmental lawyer shall not, without prior judicial approval, subpoena an attorney to appear before a grand jury or other tribunal investigating criminal activity in circumstances where the prosecutor or other governmental lawyer seeks to compel the attorney/witness to provide evidence concerning a person who is or has been represented by the attorney/witness.

TRANSACTIONS WITH PERSONS OTHER THAN CLIENTS

RULE 4.1 Truthfulness in Statements to Others

In the course of representing a client a lawyer shall not knowingly:

(a) make a false statement of material fact or law to a third person; or

(b) fail to disclose a material fact to a third person when disclosure is necessary to avoid aiding or abetting a criminal or fraudulent act by a client, unless disclosure is prohibited by Rule 1.6.

RULE 4.2 Communication With Person Represented by Counsel

In representing a client, a lawyer shall not communicate about the subject of the representation with a party the lawyer knows to be represented by another lawyer in the matter, unless the lawyer has the consent of the other lawyer or is authorized by law to do so.

RULE 4.3 Dealing with Unrepresented Person and Communicating with One of Adverse Interest

(a) In dealing on behalf of a client with a person who is not represented by counsel, a lawyer shall not state or imply that the lawyer is disinterested.

(b) During the course of a lawyer's representation of a client, a lawyer shall not give advice to a person who is not represented by a lawyer, other than the advice to secure counsel, if the interests of such person are or have a reasonable possibility of being in conflict with the interests of the lawyer's client.

(c) When the lawyer knows or reasonably should know that the unrepresented person misunderstands the lawyer's role in the matter, the lawyer should make reasonable efforts to correct the misunderstanding.

RULE 4.4 Respect for Rights of Third Persons

In representing a client, a lawyer shall not use methods of obtaining evidence that violate the legal rights of a third person.

LAW FIRMS AND ASSOCIATIONS

RULE 5.1 Responsibilities of a Partner or Supervisory Lawyer

(a) A partner in a law firm should make reasonable efforts to ensure that the firm has measures in effect giving reasonable assurance that all lawyers in the firm conform to the Rules of Professional Conduct.

(b) A lawyer having direct supervisory authority over another lawyer should make reasonable efforts to ensure that the other lawyer conforms to the Rules of Professional Conduct.

(c) A lawyer shall be responsible for another lawyer's violation of the Rules of Professional Conduct if:

(1) the lawyer orders or, with knowledge of the specific conduct, ratifies the conduct involved; or

(2) the lawyer is a partner in the law firm in which the other lawyer practices, or has direct supervisory authority over the other lawyer, and knows of the conduct at a time when its consequences can be avoided or mitigated but fails to take reasonable remedial action.

RULE 5.2 Responsibilities of a Subordinate Lawyer

(a) A lawyer is bound by the Rules of Professional Conduct even when the lawyer acts at the direction of another person.

(b) A subordinate lawyer does not violate the Rules of Professional Conduct if that lawyer acts in accordance with a supervisory lawyer's reasonable resolution of an arguable question of professional duty.

RULE 5.3 Responsibilities Regarding Nonlawyer Assistants

With respect to a nonlawyer employed or retained by or associated with a lawyer:

(a) a partner in a law firm should make reasonable efforts to ensure that the firm has measures in effect giving reasonable assurance that the person's conduct is compatible with the professional obligations of the lawyer;

(b) a lawyer having direct supervisory authority over the nonlawyer shall make reasonable efforts to ensure that the person's conduct is compatible with the professional obligations of the lawyer; and

(c) a lawyer shall be responsible for conduct of such a person that would be a violation of the Rules of Professional Conduct if engaged in by a lawyer if:

(1) the lawyer orders or, with the knowledge of the specific conduct, ratifies the conduct involved; or

(2) the lawyer is a partner in the law firm in which the person is employed, or has direct supervisory authority over the person, and knows of the conduct at a time when its consequences can be avoided or mitigated but fails to take reasonable remedial action.

RULE 5.4 Professional Independence of a Lawyer

(a) A lawyer or law firm shall not share legal fees with a nonlawyer, except that:

(1) an agreement by a lawyer with the lawyer's firm, partner, or associate may provide for the payment of money, over a reasonable period of time after the lawyer's death, to the lawyer's estate or to one or more specified persons;

(2) a lawyer who undertakes to complete unfinished legal business of a deceased lawyer may pay to the estate of the deceased lawyer that proportion of the total compensation which fairly represents the services rendered by the deceased lawyer; and

(3) a lawyer or law firm may include nonlawyer employees in a compensation or retirement plan, even though the plan is based in whole or in part on a profit-sharing arrangement.

(b) A lawyer shall not form a partnership with a nonlawyer if any of the activities of the partnership consist of the practice of law.

(c) A lawyer shall not permit a person who recommends, employs, or pays the lawyer to render legal services for another to direct or regulate the lawyer's professional judgment in rendering such legal services.

(d) A lawyer shall not practice with or in the form of a professional corporation or association authorized to practice law for a profit, if:

(1) a nonlawyer owns any interest therein, except that a fiduciary representative of the estate of a lawyer may hold the stock or interest of the lawyer for a reasonable time during administration;

(2) a nonlawyer is a corporate director or officer thereof; or

(3) a nonlawyer has the right to direct or control the professional judgment of a lawyer.

RULE 5.5 Unauthorized Practice of Law

A lawyer shall not:

(a) aid a nonlawyer in the unauthorized practice of law; or

(b) practice law in a jurisdiction where to do so would be in violation of regulations of the profession in that jurisdiction.

RULE 5.6 Restrictions on Right to Practice

A lawyer shall not participate in offering or making:

(a) a partnership or employment agreement that restricts the rights of a lawyer to practice after termination of the relationship, except an agreement concerning benefits upon retirement; or

(b) an agreement in which a restriction on the lawyer's right to practice is part of the settlement of a controversy between private parties.

PUBLIC SERVICE

RULE 6.1 Pro Bono Publico Service

A lawyer should render public interest legal service. A lawyer may discharge this responsibility by providing professional services at no fee or a reduced fee to persons of limited means or to public service or charitable groups or organizations, by service in activities for improving the law, the legal system or the legal profession, and by financial support for organizations that provide legal services to persons of limited means.

RULE 6.2 Accepting Appointments

A lawyer shall not seek to avoid appointment by a tribunal to represent a person except for good cause, such as:

(a) representing the client is likely to result in violation of the Rules of Professional Conduct or other law;

(b) representing the client is likely to result in an unreasonable financial burden on the lawyer; or

(c) the client or the cause is so repugnant to the lawyer as to be likely to impair the client-lawyer relationship or the lawyer's ability to represent the client.

RULE 6.3 Membership in Legal Services Organization

A lawyer may serve as a director, officer or member of a legal services organization, apart from the law firm in which the lawyer practices, notwithstanding that the organization serves persons having interests adverse to a client of the lawyer. The lawyer shall not knowingly participate in a decision or action of the organization:

(a) if participating in the decision would be incompatible with the lawyer's obligations to a client under Rule 1.7; or

(b) where the decision could have a material adverse effect on the representation of a client of the organization whose interests are adverse to a client of the lawyer.

RULE 6.4 Law Reform Activities Affecting Client Interests

A lawyer may serve as a director, officer or member of an organization involved in reform of the law or its administration notwithstanding that the reform may affect the interests of a client of the lawyer. When the lawyer knows that the interests of a client may be materially benefitted by a decision in which the lawyer participates, the lawyer shall disclose that fact but need not identify the client.

INFORMATION ABOUT LEGAL SERVICES

RULE 7.1 Communications Concerning a Lawyer's Services

A lawyer shall not make a false or misleading communication about the lawyer or the lawyer's services. A communication is false or misleading if it:

(a) contains a material misrepresentation of fact or law, or omits a fact necessary to make the statement considered as a whole not materially misleading;

(b) is likely to create an unjustified expectation about results the lawyer can achieve, or states or implies that the lawyer can achieve results by means that violate the rules of professional conduct or other law; or

(c) compares the lawyer's services with other lawyers' services, unless the comparison can be factually substantiated.

RULE 7.2 Advertising

(a) Subject to the requirements of Rule 7.1, a lawyer may advertise services through public media, such as a telephone directory, legal directory, newspaper or other periodical, outdoor, radio or television, or through written communication not within the purview of Rule 7.3.

(b) A copy or recording of an advertisement or written communication shall be kept for two years after its last dissemination along with a record of when and where it was used. This record shall include the name of at least one lawyer responsible for its content.

(c) A lawyer shall not give anything of value to a person for recommending the lawyer's services, except that a lawyer may pay the reasonable cost of advertising or written communication permitted by this rule and may pay the usual charges of a not-for-profit lawyer referral service or other legal service organization.

RULE 7.3. Direct Contact with Prospective Clients

(a) A lawyer [may] shall not solicit in-person or by intermediary professional employment from a prospective client with whom the lawyer has no family or prior professional relationship when a significant move for the lawyer's doing so is the lawyer's pecuniary gain. The term "solicit" includes contact in person or by telephone, but, subject to the requirements of Rule 7.1 and Rule 7.3(b), does not include written communications, which may include targeted, direct mail advertisements.

(b) A lawyer shall not contact, or send a written communication to, a prospective client for the purpose of obtaining professional employment if:

(1) the lawyer knows or reasonably should know that the physical, emotional or mental state of the person is such that the person could not exercise reasonable judgment in employing a lawyer;

(2) the person has made known to the lawyer a desire not to receive communications from the lawyer; or

(3) the communication involves coercion, duress, or harassment.

RULE 7.4 Communication of Fields of Practice

A lawyer may communicate the fact that the lawyer does or does not practice in particular fields of law. A lawyer shall not state that the lawyer is a specialist except as follows:

(a) a lawyer admitted to engage in patent practice before the United States Patent and Trademark Office may use the designation "patent attorney" or a substantially similar designation;

(b) a lawyer engaged in admiralty practice may use the designation "admiralty," "proctor in admiralty" or a substantially similar designation.

RULE 7.5 Firm Names and Letterheads

(a) A lawyer shall not use a firm name, letterhead or other professional designation that violates Rule 7.1. A trade name may be used by a lawyer in private practice if it does not imply a connection with a government, agency government, or with a public or charitable legal services organization and is not otherwise in violation of Rule 7.1. If otherwise lawful a firm may use as, or continue to include in, its name, the name or names of one or more deceased or retired members of the firm or of a predecessor firm in a continuing line of succession.

(b) A law firm with offices in more than one jurisdiction may use the same name in each jurisdiction, but identification of the lawyers in an office of the firm shall indicate the jurisdictional limitations on those not licensed to practice in the jurisdiction where the office is located.

(c) The name of a lawyer holding a public office shall not be used in the name of a law firm, or in communications on its behalf, during any substantial period in which the lawyer is not actively and regularly practicing with the firm.

(d) Lawyers shall not state or imply that they practice in a partnership or other organization only when that is the fact.

MAINTAINING THE INTEGRITY OF THE PROFESSION

RULE 8.1 Bar Admission and Disciplinary Matters

(a) A lawyer is subject to discipline if the lawyer has made a materially false statement in, or if the lawyer has deliberately failed to disclose a material fact requested in connection with, the lawyer's application for admission to the bar or any disciplinary matter.

(b) A lawyer shall not further the application for admission to the bar of another person known by the lawyer to be unqualified in respect to character, education, or other relevant attribute.

RULE 8.2 Statements Concerning Judges and Other Adjudicatory Officers

(a) A lawyer shall not knowingly make false statements of fact concerning the qualifications of a candidate for election or appointment to a judicial office.

(b) A lawyer shall not knowingly make false accusations against a judge or other adjudicatory officers.

(c) A lawyer who is a candidate for judicial office shall comply with the applicable provisions of Canon 7 of the Code of Judicial Conduct.

RULE 8.3 Reporting Professional Misconduct

(a) A lawyer having knowledge that another lawyer has committed a violation of the Rules of Professional Conduct that raises a substantial question as to that lawyer's honesty, trustworthiness or fitness as a lawyer in other respects, shall inform the appropriate professional authority.

(b) A lawyer having knowledge that a judge has committed a violation of applicable rules of judicial conduct that raises a substantial question as to the judge's fitness for office shall inform the appropriate authority.

(c) This rule does not require disclosure of information otherwise protected by Rule 1.6.

RULE 8.4 Misconduct

It is professional misconduct for a lawyer to:

(a) violate or attempt to violate the Rules of Professional Conduct, knowingly assist or induce another to do so, or do so through the acts of another;

(b) commit a criminal act that reflects adversely on the lawyer's honesty, trustworthiness or fitness as a lawyer in other respects;

(c) engage in conduct involving dishonesty, fraud, deceit or misrepresentation;

(d) engage in conduct that is prejudicial to the administration of justice;

(e) state or imply an ability to influence improperly a government agency or official; or

(f) knowingly assist a judge or judicial officer in conduct that is a violation of applicable rules of judicial conduct or other law.

RULE 8.5 Jurisdiction

A lawyer admitted to practice in this jurisdiction is subject to the disciplinary authority of this jurisdiction although engaged in practice elsewhere.

Index

Index

Index